wacky
baby
knits

wacky baby knits

20 Knitted Designs for the Fashion-Conscious Toddler

Alison Jenkins

PERIGEE

A PERIGEE BOOK
Published by the Penguin Group
Penguin Group (USA) Inc.
375 Hudson Street, New York, New York 10014, USA
Penguin Group (Canada), 90 Eglinton Avenue East,
Suite 700, Toronto, Ontario M4P 2Y3, Canada
(a division of Pearson Penguin Canada Inc.)
Penguin Books Ltd., 80 Strand, London WC2R 0RL, England
Penguin Group Ireland, 25 St. Stephen's Green, Dublin 2, Ireland
(a division of Penguin Books Ltd.)
Penguin Group (Australia), 250 Camberwell Road, Camberwell, Victoria
3124, Australia (a division of Pearson Australia Group Pty. Ltd.)
Penguin Books India Pvt. Ltd., 11 Community Centre,
Panchsheel Park, New Delhi—110 017, India
Penguin Group (NZ), 67 Apollo Drive, Rosedale, North Shore 0632,
New Zealand (a division of Pearson New Zealand Ltd.)
Penguin Books (South Africa) (Pty.) Ltd., 24 Sturdee Avenue,
Rosebank, Johannesburg 2196, South Africa

Penguin Books Ltd., Registered Offices: 80 Strand,
London WC2R 0RL, England

While the author has made every effort to provide accurate telephone
numbers and Internet addresses at the time of publication, neither the
publisher nor the author assumes any responsibility for errors, or for
changes that occur after publication. Further, the publisher does not have
any control over and does not assume any responsibility for author or third-
party websites or their content.

THIS BOOK WAS CONCEIVED, DESIGNED, AND PRODUCED BY
Ivy Press
210 High Street
Lewes, East Sussex
BN7 2NS, UK
www.ivy-group.co.uk

CREATIVE DIRECTOR Peter Bridgewater
PUBLISHER Jason Hook
EDITORIAL DIRECTOR Tom Kitch
SENIOR EDITOR Lorraine Turner
ART DIRECTOR Wayne Blades
DESIGN Clare Barber, Kate Haynes
ILLUSTRATIONS Melvyn Evans
PHOTOGRAPHER Andrew Perris

Library of Congress Cataloging-in-Publication Data

Jenkins, Alison.
Wacky Baby Knits: 20 Knitted Designs for the Fashion-Conscious Toddler /
Alison Jenkins.
  p. cm
"A Perigee Book."
Includes index.
ISBN: 978-0-399-53503-1
1. Knitting—Patterns. 2. Infants' clothing. I. Title.
TT825.J42845 2009
746.43'20432—dc22   2008054668

PRINTED IN THAILAND

10 9 8 7 6 5 4 3 2 1

Most Perigee books are available at special quantity discounts for bulk
purchases for sales promotions, premiums, fund-raising, or educational
use. Special books, or book excerpts, can also be created to fit specific
needs. For details, write: Special Markets, Penguin Group (USA) Inc.,
375 Hudson Street, New York, New York 10014.

SAFETY NOTE

Some of these garments have small parts, such as buttons and
decorations, that could be harmful to babies. For safety reasons, it
is therefore very important to ensure that these are attached to the
knitted garments securely. If in doubt, omit the item in question or
replace it with a secure alternative. Seek competent and qualified
advice if necessary.

Contents

Introduction

One of the many joys of having babies is that you can dress them up in any way you choose. Sadly, this state of affairs is temporary: in a few short years they will have as many opinions about what they will and won't wear as you do. Try getting a three-year-old to wear a cute cow suit if he or she doesn't want to! Take full advantage of the opportunity while it lasts, using this book as your guide and inspiration.

Knitting for babies can be great fun and—important to a busy parent—it's quick to do. Most pattern pieces are small and don't take long to complete. Furthermore, the designs don't use much yarn and are therefore inexpensive to make. You can even use leftovers for many of the projects, which means that you can afford to be a little frivolous.

The designs are not difficult to make: None is beyond the reach and skills of a beginner. We've included some basic how-to-knit advice for true novices, plus a few hints and tips about making up the patterns to give them a neat and professional finish. Every design has full instructions, plus pattern charts where required. All you need to get started are knitting needles and a few balls of yarn—and a little bit of time, of course, which admittedly can be at a premium with a baby in the home.

All babies display different personalities, but this book aims to provide simple, colorful, and cute designs to suit any baby from head to toe. Why not try making an Elvis Hat, a Tiny Biker Jacket, a Cow Suit with Horned Hat, or Monster Boots and Mitts to match? Or what about a Cupcake Hat or a Ballet Top with Tulle Tutu? Or perhaps a Mohawk Hat or Pirate Suit with a matching hat would be more suitable for your little one?

Whether you are knitting an outfit for everyday wear, for a special birthday or costume party, or just for fun, remember to keep a camera on hand to make a photographic record of your baby's funky infant days—the pictures are sure to provide you with hours of entertainment in the future when baby grows up.

Baby Knit Basics

Basic Equipment

You will need very little equipment in order to knit any of the funky baby knits projects contained in this book. Two pairs of needles, a ball of yarn, and a nice fat bodkin fulfill the basic requirements. There are, however, a few more bits and pieces that will make your funky knitting life a little easier: see the list here for suggestions.

Needles

Knitting needles can be made from plastic, metal, wood, or bamboo. Each has a blunt point at one end, and a knob at the other, to prevent the stitches from falling off.

NEEDLE SIZE CHART

You can often find a suggested needle size on the label of the yarn you are buying. However, you should always knit a test sample first, to check the gauge of your knitting.

US	METRIC
0	2 mm
1	2.25 mm
2	2.75 mm
3	3.25 mm
4	3.5 mm
5	3.75 mm
6	4 mm
7	4.5 mm
8	5 mm
9	5.5 mm
10	6 mm
10½	6.5, 7, 7.5 mm
11	8 mm
13	9 mm
15	10 mm
17	12 mm
19	16 mm
35	19 mm
50	25 mm

CHOOSING YOUR NEEDLES

Only two sizes of needle have been used for the projects in this book: size 3 (3.25 mm) and size 6 (4 mm).

A circular needle is also useful. This comprises two short knitting needles without knobs at the ends, joined together with a flexible plastic cord. Use this to work on lots of stitches at the same time; for example, around a hood edge, or on a curve such as a neckline.

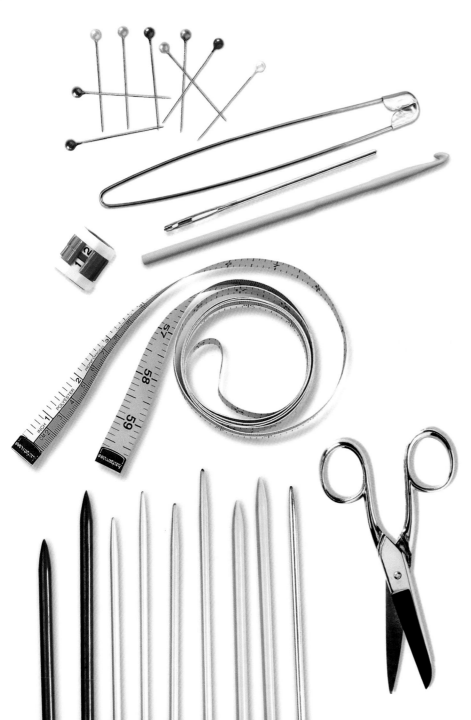

Other equipment

BODKIN
This is a fat needle with a large eye and a blunt point. Use it to sew your knitted pieces together. Don't use an ordinary needle—the eye is too small, and the sharp point will snag the yarn.

CROCHET HOOK
A crochet hook is a very useful tool for picking up dropped stitches.

PINS
Use pins for marking gauge swatches and for pinning garment pieces together. Use only large pins with glass heads to prevent them from getting lost in the knitting. Remove all pins when you have finished stitching the pieces together.

ROW COUNTER
A row counter is a really useful little device. Slide it onto the end of your needle, and leave it there for the duration of your knitting. As you finish each row, you simply adjust the number of rows shown on the row counter to help you remember how many rows you have knitted.

RULER
Use a rigid plastic ruler for measuring gauge.

SMALL SCISSORS
Keep a pair of small, sharp embroidery scissors handy for snipping off yarn ends.

STITCH HOLDER
This looks like a giant safety pin. Keep a few of them on hand because they are very useful for holding stitches that are not in use.

TAPE MEASURE
This is used for making general measurements.

Yarn Essentials

There are many different criteria for choosing yarn. Color is important, but texture is very important too, because baby's sensitive skin can easily be irritated by prickly, tickly fibers. And is it washable? Dry-clean or specialist-wash yarns are not really practical for use in baby garments.

Choosing yarn

There are lots of different weights and styles of yarn available in most stores but, for the purposes of this book, we've kept it really simple. Most of the designs you will see in the following pages use basic worsted-weight (double knit) yarn, the exceptions being the Davy Crockett Hat and Furry Bear Feet, both of which use a fur-effect yarn, and the Monster Boots and Mitts, which use a textured worsted.

We've used just two sizes of needle, however, so you will not need loads of fancy equipment. Some of the smaller projects, such as bootees and hats, use very little yarn, so check the yarn quantity advice given for each pattern before you make any special yarn purchases. You may just have enough yarn left over from another project that you can use.

YARN TIPS

✿ Since dye shades can vary, when buying yarn be sure to check that each ball of yarn has the same dye lot number printed on the label, and buy enough to ensure that you can complete the garment without having to mix yarn with different dye lot numbers.

✿ If the yarn recommended by your pattern is not available, you can substitute it with a different yarn, but make sure that it is still the same weight and gauge.

✿ It is useful to keep a small quantity of leftover yarn, and the yarn label, for future reference after you have finished the garment. You will also find these useful for when you are cleaning the garment or if you need to do repairs.

Gauge

It is very important that your stitch gauge is correct. If it is too tight or too loose, then the finished garment may turn out smaller or larger than required. Make a sample before you start your actual project, using the suggested yarn and the larger size of needles indicated in the pattern. Knit a swatch of stockinette stitch (see note on page 17) about 5 in (12.5 cm) square, then mark out an area 4 in (10 cm) both horizontally and vertically with pins. Count the rows and stitches to make sure that they match the gauge given in the pattern. If not, use a larger or smaller needles size (for both sets of needles), as appropriate.

KNIT GAUGE CHART

Here is an at-a-glance guide to help you calculate yarn weight against needle size and number of stitches. Remember that this is only a guide—you should always test-knit a sample before you begin the actual garment.

YARN	NEEDLE SIZE	STITCHES (BY 4 IN [10 CM] SQUARE)
LIGHTWEIGHT		
2- and 3-ply, baby	1–5 (2.25–3.75 mm)	29–32 stitches
4- and 5-ply, baby, sport	1–5 (2.25–3.75 mm)	25–28 stitches
MEDIUM-WEIGHT		
Double knit (dk), light worsted	5–7 (3.75–4.5 mm)	21–24 stitches
Worsted, Afghan, Aran	7–9 (4.5–5.5 mm)	16–20 stitches
HEAVYWEIGHT OR BULKY		
Chunky, craft	9–11 (5.5–8 mm)	12–15 stitches
SUPER BULKY		
Roving, bulky, novelty yarns	13–19 (9–16 mm)	6–11 stitches

Start Knitting

Knitting is easy once you get the hang of it. These simple instructions show you how to hold the needles and the yarn, make a slip knot, and cast on using the thumb method. All these are suitable for beginners, and all the projects that follow use just basic knit and purl stitches, with nothing fancy hidden anywhere—that's a promise!

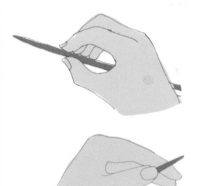

Holding the needles

RIGHT HAND
Hold the needle as shown: the thumb, index finger, and middle finger of your right hand will control the tip of the knitting needle. The other fingers stabilize the needle as you work.

LEFT HAND
The needle is held in a similar position to the right hand.

Holding the yarn

Holding the yarn correctly is essential in order to achieve an even gauge throughout your knitted work. Pass the yarn over the index finger of your right hand, under the middle finger, then over the ring finger, as shown. The little finger controls the tension, and the index finger manipulates the yarn to form the stitches.

NOTE: For left-handers, simply reverse the holding positions.

Making a slip knot

Having mastered the art of needle-holding, you may now begin to cast on stitches. Making a slip knot is the first step: this knot is counted as the first stitch in a cast-on row and also secures the yarn to the needle.

1

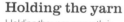

Unwind enough yarn from the ball for the number of stitches required, plus an extra 12 in (30 cm), and hold it in your left hand: this end of the yarn is called a "tail." As a guide to the correct amount, 6 in (15 cm) of yarn is enough to knit approximately 10 stitches. Wind the yarn twice around your index and middle fingers, then use the tip of the needle to pull the first strand through the second.

2 Use the needle to ease the strand out to form a loop, then adjust the tail and the yarn attached to the ball, called "the working yarn," so the loop fits snugly around the needle.

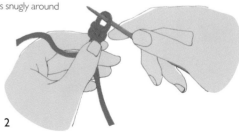

2

Simple cast-on using the thumb method

Casting on can be a tricky technique to master, but it really is important that you get it right. Practice makes perfect. If you're a novice knitter, make sure that you are confident with casting on before you begin the actual garment. Use this method to cast on an elastic row of stitches that will form the first row of your knitted garment.

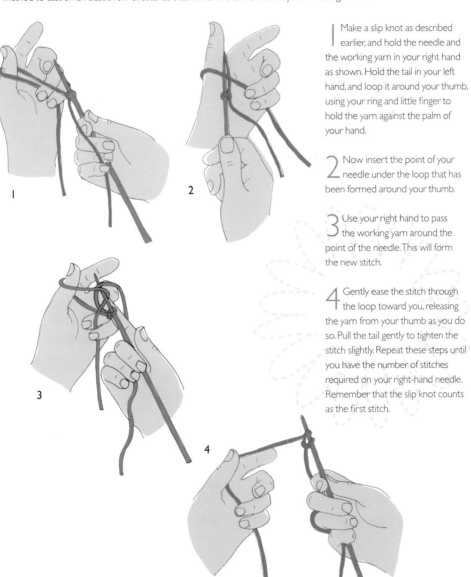

1 Make a slip knot as described earlier, and hold the needle and the working yarn in your right hand as shown. Hold the tail in your left hand, and loop it around your thumb, using your ring and little finger to hold the yarn against the palm of your hand.

2 Now insert the point of your needle under the loop that has been formed around your thumb.

3 Use your right hand to pass the working yarn around the point of the needle. This will form the new stitch.

4 Gently ease the stitch through the loop toward you, releasing the yarn from your thumb as you do so. Pull the tail gently to tighten the stitch slightly. Repeat these steps until you have the number of stitches required on your right-hand needle. Remember that the slip knot counts as the first stitch.

USEFUL TIP

If you find that you have overestimated the yarn and that the "tail" is quite long after you have completed your cast-on row, do not be tempted to cut it off. Simply fold the tail in half, then in half again, then tie it in a loose knot. The yarn will be useful for sewing up seams later when the garment is completed.

Basic Knitting

You should now have the required number of stitches on your needle and will no doubt be keen to get knitting. First you must learn two knitting basics: the knit stitch and the purl stitch. If you master these, then you can do just about anything.

Using knit stitch

The knit stitch is the easiest stitch to master, and is usually abbreviated to "k" in your knitting pattern.

KNIT STITCH

1 Transfer the needle holding the cast-on stitches to your left hand, and hold the other needle in your right hand. Place the point of the right-hand needle through the first cast-on stitch from front to back, as shown.

2 Take up the working yarn in your right hand (make sure that the yarn is passed over your fingers correctly to ensure an even gauge), then use your index finger to guide it around the point of the left-hand needle.

3 Holding the right-hand needle and the working yarn firmly, draw the resulting loop gently back through the first stitch.

4 Ease the right-hand needle away from the work slightly, to allow the first stitch of the cast-on row to slip off the left-hand needle. The first knit stitch is complete.

5 Repeat steps one through four to the end of the row.

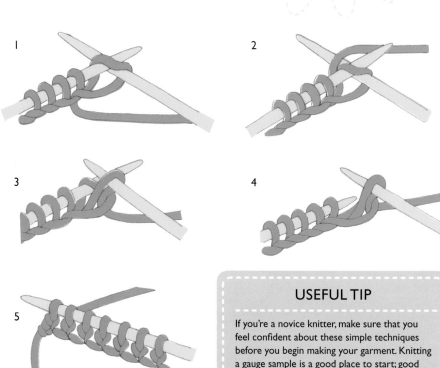

USEFUL TIP

If you're a novice knitter, make sure that you feel confident about these simple techniques before you begin making your garment. Knitting a gauge sample is a good place to start; good practice for casting on, knit and purl, binding off, and maintaining a uniform gauge.

Using purl stitch

The purl stitch is a little more tricky to master than the knit stitch, but still fairly simple. It is usually abbreviated to "p" in your knitting pattern.

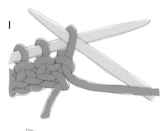

I

2

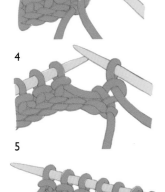

3

4

5

PURL STITCH

1 Transfer the needle with the first row of knit stitches to your left hand in order to begin the purl row. Place the point of your right-hand needle through the first stitch from back to front, as shown.

2 Guide the working yarn around the point of the right-hand needle using the index finger of your right hand.

3 Carefully draw the resulting loop back through the first stitch, to form the beginning of the purl row.

4 Ease the right-hand needle away from the work slightly, to allow the first stitch of the previous row to slip off the left-hand needle, thus beginning the first purl row.

5 Repeat steps one through four, purling all the stitches in the same way until you reach the end of the row. All the stitches will now have been transferred from the left-hand needle to the right-hand needle.

NOTE: Knit and purl rows worked alternately are referred to as "stockinette stitch." The right side is smooth and the wrong side looks like rows of little bumps. Reverse stockinette stitch is worked the same way, but the purl (bumpy) side is used as the right side.

Ribbing

Most knitted garments begin and end with a band of ribbing as a way to create a neat and elastic edge. Rib bands are also used for button bands. The following steps show you how to work single ribbing, which is simply a row of knit and purl stitches worked alternately.

SINGLE RIBBING

Single ribbing is often abbreviated to: "k1, p1 rib."

1 Cast on the required number of stitches, then work in rib as follows: knit the first stitch, then bring the working yarn to the front of the work between the first and second stitches; purl the second stitch.

2 Now take the working yarn to the back of the work between the second and third stitches, and knit the third stitch.

3 Continue in this way, knitting and purling alternately, until you reach the end of the cast-on row. For the next row of ribbing, purl all the knit stitches and knit all the purl stitches.

NOTE: Some patterns require the rib row to begin with a purl stitch.

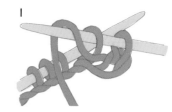

I

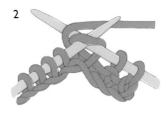

2

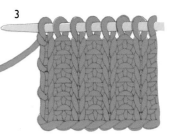

3

OTHER RIBBING METHODS

Ribbing can be done by working more than one alternate knit and purl stitch (for example, two knit stitches and two purl stitches form "double rib"). Most designs in this book, however, use single rib, apart from the Cupcake Hat, which uses two knit stitches and one purl stitch in sequence.

Increasing and Decreasing

Increasing and decreasing stitches help you to shape pieces of knitting (such as sleeves or necklines) to fit the body. Our designs use the one-stitch increase and decrease methods. In general, where the increase takes place at the end or beginning of a row, it is positioned one stitch in from the edge unless the pattern states otherwise.

Increasing by one stitch

Increasing by one stitch is usually abbreviated to "inc 1 st." The decorative method of increasing one stitch by picking up the loop between stitches is abbreviated to "m 1," and is shown below.

1

2
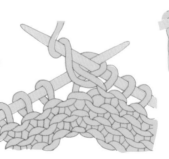

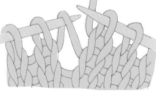

1 To increase one stitch in a knit row, knit to the point of increase (your pattern will indicate number of stitches). Knit the next stitch, but do not slip it off the needle as usual; instead, knit into the back of it, as shown, to create a new stitch. Now slip the double stitch off the needle.

2 To increase one stitch in a purl row, purl to the indicated point of increase. Purl the next stitch, but do not slip it off the needle; instead take the yarn to the back of the work, then knit into the back of the stitch, as shown. Slip the double stitch off the needle.

NOTE: You can also increase a stitch simply by knitting into the loop that lies between two stitches. This makes a decorative hole in the work and is used on Pointy Slippers. This method is used on knit rows.

Decreasing by one stitch

Decreasing one stitch is usually abbreviated to:"dec 1 st," or "k2tog" (knit two stitches together) or "p2tog" (purl two stitches together).

KNIT ROW

To decrease one stitch in a knit row, work to the point of decrease, then knit the next two stitches together. This causes a visible slant to the right on the right side of your work, and should be used at the end of a row.

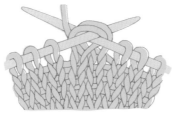

PURL ROW

To decrease one stitch in a purl row, work to the point of decrease, then purl two stitches together, as shown. This causes a visible slant to the left on the right side of the work and should be used at the start of a row.

Slip stitch decrease

Use this method of decreasing at the beginning of a row because it creates a visible slant to the left on the right side of the work.

1 Knit to the indicated point of decrease, and slip the next stitch off the left-hand needle and onto the right-hand needle. Knit the next stitch.

1

2 Use the tip of the left-hand needle to lift the slipped stitch over the knitted stitch. Continue to work to the end of the row.

2

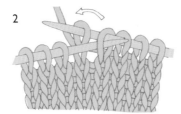

Decorative Techniques

Color-changing techniques take a little practice, but are worth it. Here, you will learn how to knit decorative effects into your work, from creating a decorative bobble, to using more than one color in the same row, whether for a vertical striped effect (Cupcake Hat), large areas of color (Cow Suit), or small motifs (Baseball Jacket).

Decorative bobble technique

This decorative bobble is used to add texture to the Frog Suit with Hood (see page 82). One stitch is worked into several times, then the extra stitches are passed over the last stitch to create a little cluster of loops which result in a bobble on the right side of the work. This is abbreviated to "mb" (make bobble) in pattern instructions.

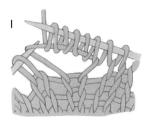

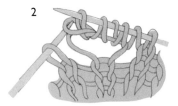

1 Work to the bobble position, purl into the next stitch, then knit into the same stitch. Repeat once more, then purl once. You have made five extra stitches.

2 Use the tip of the left-hand needle to pass the first four extra stitches over the last to form the looped bobble. Work to the next bobble position, and repeat.

Fair Isle method

This method should be used if the colors you intend to add in the row do not exceed three or four stitches at a time. The different-colored yarns are simply carried loosely at the back of the work when not in use. These loose strands are referred to as "floats." Care must be taken not to pull the floats too tightly as this might cause the finished knitting to lose elasticity.

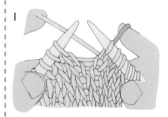

1 Work to the point of the color change, then introduce the required contrast-colored yarn, allowing the first yarn to hang at the back of the work. Work the number of stitches indicated in the pattern in the contrast yarn, then change back to the original color.

2 Strand the original yarn loosely across the back of your work while you use the contrast yarn, then do likewise with the contrast yarn while you work with the original color. Continue to the end of the row, changing colors as required. Any tails of yarn left hanging are neatly woven in later (see page 25).

Intarsia method

This is the neatest method of creating large areas of contrast color, with no long floats on the reverse side to deal with. This is especially useful for a baby garment, where those little fingers can become tangled so easily in loose threads. Each area is knitted using a separate ball of yarn, but the yarns are twisted together on the reverse side of each intersection, so that the work holds together in one piece.

DIAGONAL COLOR CHANGES

For color changes to the left or right, simply work one more or one fewer stitch in the original color before changing to the contrast yarn.

ON WRONG SIDE

This diagram shows the wrong side of a diagonal color change leading to the left on the right side. You will see yarn A linked with yarn B.

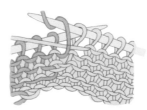

ON RIGHT SIDE

For a diagonal color change leading to the right on the right side, simply work one stitch fewer in the first yarn A, then continue in the contrast color. The two yarns will link on the wrong side because of the pattern direction.

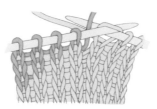

VERTICAL COLOR CHANGES

In this example, the yarns are still linked on the wrong side, but in a vertical direction.

ON RIGHT SIDE

Work the required number of stitches in yarn A, then let it fall over yarn B at the back. Take up yarn B, work required number of stitches, then change back to A. Remember to use separate balls of yarn.

ON WRONG SIDE

The required number of stitches have been worked in yarn A, then changed to yarn B, then changed back to A. The yarns have been twisted on the back to prevent holes from forming.

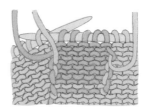

Duplicate stitch

Sometimes referred to as "Swiss embroidery" or "darning," duplicate stitch is worked by hand when the garment is complete and is so called because it imitates stockinette stitch on the right side of a knitted piece. This method is useful when adding small areas of color or small motifs.

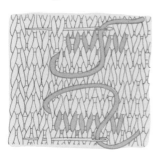

1 Indicate the position of the motif on the right side of the garment using pins if necessary. Now thread a bodkin with your contrast-colored yarn, and secure the end on the reverse side. Bring the needle out at the base of the stitch at the lower right-hand corner of the design or motif. Now insert the needle from left to right, under the base of the next stitch above, and pull the yarn through gently.

2 Reinsert the needle into the base of the first stitch from left to right again, to form the first embroidered stitch. Continue in this way to complete the embroidered pattern or motif.

NOTE: You will find colored charts included with your knitting instructions that relate to patterns and motifs (see Cow Suit with Horned Hat, and Baseball Jacket).

How to make a pom-pom

Pom-poms make versatile, eye-catching decorations, and are easy to make.

1 Cut two circles of card, each a little larger than the diameter of your finished pom-pom. Cut a small hole in the center of each., to make a donut shape. Sandwich the two circles together, aligning the holes in the middle. Start winding yarn around the outside and through the hole, working your way around the circle, until the inner hole is filled with yarn.

2 Slide a pair of scissors between the two pieces of cardboard, and cut through the loops around the outside of the circles. Pull the circles apart, then tie a 16 in (40 cm) length of yarn tightly around the center, leaving the ends of the yarn free to attach the pom-pom to the garment. Remove the card circles, and trim the pom-pom so that it is even.

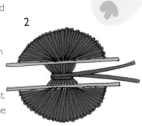

How to make a yarn button

A pretty alternative to store-bought buttons, yarn buttons are soft to the touch, too, so won't be uncomfortable for baby to wear. This method creates a tight spherical button—you may need to practice the technique a little to get it right.

1

2

1 For each button, cut 3–5 strands of yarn, each approximately 10 in (25 cm) long, depending on the size of button required. Make the first simple loop as shown, passing the right-hand end over the left.

2 Make the second loop by passing the right-hand end over the first loop and under the left-hand end as shown. Remember to keep the yarn quite loose at this stage.

3

4

3 To complete the basic form of the button, pass the right-hand end over and under the yarn at the center in order to secure the loops.

4 Gently pull the ends of the yarn to draw the loops together into a tight knot. Tie the ends together, and use the yarn to sew onto the garment to correspond with the buttonholes.

HOW TO PICK UP A DROPPED STITCH

It's really annoying to see a dropped stitch in your knitting, especially if you don't notice until you're nearly finished! Don't despair: it can easily be fixed with the use of a crochet hook.

1 The dropped stitch will look like a little ladder working its way down to the bottom of your knitting. It's a good idea to catch the stitch using a safety pin while you locate your crochet hook, to prevent it from travelling even farther.

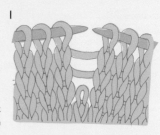

2 Simply insert the crochet hook into the dropped stitch, then pick up the loop that lies between the stitches on the next row up.

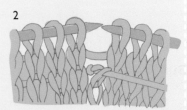

3 Pull the loop back through the dropped stitch, then repeat step 2. Continue until you reach the top of the ladder, then slip the stitch onto the needle. All fixed.

Binding Off

All stitches must be secured when you get to the end of a knitted piece (unless you are transferring them to a stitch holder to be worked on later). This is called "binding off." Three methods are given here: binding off on a knit row, a purl row, or for a ribbed band.

Binding off knitwise

Always bind off in this way if you are binding off a knit row with the right side facing. Note: Use this when binding off reverse stockinette stitch from the right side.

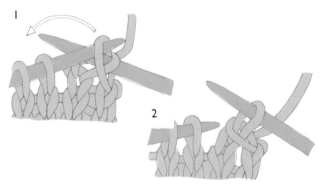

1 Knit the first two stitches of the bind-off row, then, using the point of your left-hand needle, pick up the first stitch and pass it over the second, thus losing (binding off) one stitch.

2 Continue working in this way until you reach the last stitch. Snip off the working yarn, and pull it through the last stitch to secure the bind-off edge.

Binding off purlwise

This method is similar to binding off knitwise, but is worked in purl instead. Be sure to bind off in this way if you are working a purl row with the wrong (purl) side facing; it gives a neat appearance from the right side of the garment. Purl the first two stitches of the row, then, using the point of your left-hand needle, pick up the first stitch and pass it over the second stitch, thus binding off one stitch. Continue in this way until you reach the last stitch. Snip off the working yarn, and pull it through the last stitch to fasten off securely.

Binding off in rib

You can bind off in single rib to produce a finished edge that is especially useful for neckbands and cuffs. This results in an elastic edge. When you reach the end of a ribbed band around a neckline or perhaps a button band, you can begin the bind-off row.

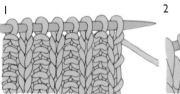

1 To bind off, work a stitch following the rib pattern of the previous rows; this may be a knit or a purl stitch. The diagram shows this as a knit stitch.

2 After the first stitch, bring the yarn to the front of the work ready to purl the next stitch. Purl this stitch in the usual way.

3 Take the yarn to the back of the work. Using the tip of your left needle, ease the first knit stitch over the second purl stitch. You have now bound off a stitch. Knit the next stitch.

4 Pass the purled stitch over the knit stitch you have just worked. Continue in this way until you have one stitch left, then snip off the yarn and pull it through the last stitch to secure.

Finishing Off Your Knitting

Many garments can be spoiled by poor finishing and sewing together, so it is worth spending a little time and effort learning to do this correctly. Do not be tempted to try to do this job in a hurry, no matter how eager you are to see the garment on the baby.

Picking up stitches on a shaped edge

Neckbands, button bands, and buttonhole bands require stitches to be picked up along the edge of a previously completed garment piece. Your pattern will indicate how many stitches you will need to pick up and at which end of the edge or opening to start. It can sometimes help to mark the center of the edge with a pin, so that you can arrange the picked-up stitches evenly on either side.

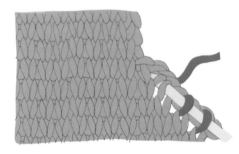

Insert the tip of your knitting needle through the work from the right side, then draw the yarn from the back to the front in the form of a loop; this forms the new stitch. Keep the loop on the needle and repeat to pick up another stitch. Continue until you have the required number of stitches on your needle. Work the next row in ribbing or as indicated in the pattern.

Eyelet buttonhole

This method creates a discreet hole suitable for a small button; it can be worked as part of the garment or included in a button band worked on an edge or into an opening. The buttonhole is begun in one row and completed in the next.

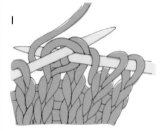

1 Work to the buttonhole position as directed in your knitting pattern, then take the working yarn forward under the point of the right-hand needle, then back over the top to the original knitting position—abbreviated to "yrn" (yarn round needle). Now knit the next two stitches together.

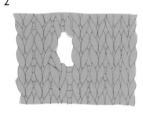

2 For the next row, work across all stitches as usual. You will see that a small hole has formed in the buttonhole position.

Sewing in tails

Unless your knitted item is very small, you will probably need to join in a new ball of yarn at some point, or perhaps change color. This results in tails of yarn hanging down on the reverse side of your work. These are messy and can work loose, so they need to be neatly secured. Do not be tempted to snip them off without securing them—otherwise your knitting will definitely unravel.

1 With the wrong side of your work facing, thread the tail onto a bodkin, and work under and over the back of four or five stitches, as shown. Stretch the knitting slightly, so that the worked yarn is not too tight.

2 As an extra safety precaution, work the tail back along the stitches in the opposite direction. Snip off the yarn about ½ in (1.5 cm) from the surface of the knitted work.

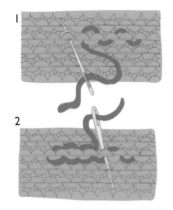

SKILL RATINGS

EASY

AVERAGE

ADVANCED

Sewing together

There are many ways to sew garment pieces together, but the invisible method is by far the best. The resulting seam is inconspicuous, elastic, and not bulky, which is especially important for small knitted items.

THE INVISIBLE SEAM
This neat way of joining seams is often referred to as "mattress stitch."

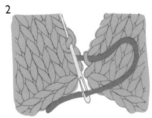

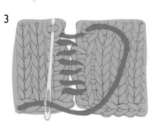

1 Place the pieces to be joined right side up and side by side. Thread a bodkin with matching yarn and secure one of the ends to the lower right-hand edge on the reverse side. Now bring the yarn through to the right side.

2 Use the point of the bodkin to pick up the center strand of the first stitch at the lower edge of the left-hand piece, and pull the yarn through. Now pick up a stitch in the same way on the right-hand piece.

3 Work along the seam, picking up one stitch at a time, first from one side, then the other, until the seam is complete. Pull the yarn gently as you go, so that the seam draws together, but not so tightly that it becomes distorted. Fasten off by working a few small stitches over the seam on the wrong side; sew in the tails (above).

Hats

Classic Beret

This little sailor can't dance the hornpipe yet but, once he has donned the appropriate headwear, anything is possible. The navy, blue, and white color scheme is a classic combination for those occasions when baby needs to look smart and shipshape. You could also make a multicolored striped beret to turn heads and make a fashion splash.

CHECKLIST

YOU WILL NEED
* pair of size 3 (3.25 mm) needles
* pair of size 6 (4 mm) needles
* 1(1:1) 2 oz (50 g) ball light worsted knitting yarn in color A (white)
* 1(1:1) 2 oz (50 g) ball light worsted knitting yarn in color B (blue)
* 1(1:1) 2 oz (50 g) ball light worsted knitting yarn in color C (navy blue)
* tape measure
* bodkin

TO FIT SIZES
0–3 months: chest 16 in (41 cm)
3–6 months: chest 18 in (46 cm)
6–12 months: chest 20 in (51cm)
NOTE: The hat is designed to fit an average sized baby's head

GAUGE
22 stitches and 30 rows to 4 in (10 cm), measured over stockinette stitch, using size 6 (4 mm) needles

Beret

Using size 3 (3.25 mm) needles and col A, cast on 69 (75: 81) sts.
Work in k1, p1 rib, following color sequence as follows:
Rib 1 row in col A.
Rib 2 rows in col C.
Rib 6 rows in col B.
Rib 2 rows in col C.
Rib 2 rows in col A.
Change to size 6 (4 mm) needles and cont in st st and col A, increasing as follows:
(k1, inc 1) 34 (37:40) times, then k1 (1: 1). There will now be 103 (112: 121) sts. Cont in st st until work measures 4 (4¼: 4¾) in [10 (11: 12) cm] from cast-on edge, ending after a ws row.

CROWN SHAPING

With rs facing, beg crown dec and cont color sequence as follows:
1st row: change to col B, k1, *k2tog, k7; rep from * to last 3 sts, then k2tog, k1.
2nd row: purl all sts.
3rd row: change to col A, k1, *k2tog, k6; rep from * to last 2 sts, then k2tog.
4th row: purl all sts.
5th row: change to col B, k1, *k2tog, k5; rep from * to last st, k1.
6th row: purl all sts.

7th row: change to col A, k1, *k2tog, k4; rep from * to last st, k1.
8th row: purl all sts.
9th row: change to col B, k1, *k2tog, k3; rep from * to last st, k1.
10th row: purl all sts.
11th row: change to col C, k1, *k2tog, k2; rep from * to last st, k1.
12th row: purl all sts.
13th row: change to col B, k1, *k2tog, k1; rep from * to last st, k1.
14th row: purl all sts.
15th row: change to col C, k1, *k2tog; rep from * to end.
16th row: purl all sts.
17th row: change to col B, k1 (0: 1), *k2tog; rep from * to end.
18th row: purl all sts.
19th row: change to col C, knit 1 row.
Work in st st for a further 4 rows, then bind off all sts.
Break off yarn and, using a bodkin, draw it through the last st to fasten off, leaving a long tail.

Sewing together

* Using matching yarn and a bodkin, stitch the beret seam. Weave in all loose ends neatly on the reverse.

Davy Crockett Hat

Whether your baby is heading out to the wild frontier of toddler gymnastics or the badlands of a play date, you know he will be toasty warm in this striking hat. He'll maintain his image while enjoying its woolly comfort—and the tail can act as a suitable diversion in idle moments during his busy day.

CHECKLIST

YOU WILL NEED

- pair of size 3 (3.25 mm) needles
- pair of size 6 (4 mm) needles
- 1 (1:1) 2 oz (50 g) ball fur-effect (light worsted-weight) knitting yarn in color A (brown)
- 1 (1:1) 2 oz (50 g) ball fur-effect (light worsted-weight) knitting yarn in color B (beige)
- tape measure
- bodkin

KEY

- Col A—fur-effect yarn in brown
- Col B—fur-effect yarn in beige

TO FIT SIZES

0–3 months: chest 16 in (41 cm)
3–6 months: chest 18 in (46 cm)
6–12 months: chest 20 in (51 cm)
NOTE: The hat is designed to fit an average sized baby's head

GAUGE

22 stitches and 30 rows to 4 in (10 cm), measured over stockinette stitch, using size 6 (4 mm) needles

Hat

Using size 3 (3.25 mm) needles and col A, cast on 91 (97: 103) sts.

Work in k1, p1 rib for 1½ in (4 cm), ending with a ws row.

Change to size 6 (4 mm) needles.

Cont in st st until work measures 4¼ (4¾: 5) in [11 (12: 13) cm] from cast-on edge, ending after a ws row.

CROWN SHAPING

1st row: k1, *k2tog, k4; rep from * to end.
Next and every alternate row: p all sts.
3rd row: k1, *k2tog, k3; rep from * to end.
5th row: k1, *k2tog, k2; rep from * to end.
7th row: k1, *k2tog, k1; rep from * to end.
9th row: k1, *k2tog; rep from * to end.
11th row: k0 (1:0), *k2tog; rep from * to end. There are now 8 (9: 9) sts. Break off yarn, leaving a 12 in (30 cm) tail, and draw the yarn through the sts on the needle, using a bodkin. Pull together tightly, and fasten off.

Tail

Using size 6 (4 mm) needles and col B, cast on 3 (3: 3) sts.

1st and every alternate row: p all sts.
2nd row: k1, m1, k1, m1, k1. (5 sts.)
4th row: k2, m1, k1, m1, k2. (7 sts.)

6th row: k3, m1, k1, m1, k3. (9 sts.)
8th row: k4, m1, k1, m1, k4. (11 sts.)
10th row: k5, m1, k1, m1, k5. (13 sts.)
12th row: k6, m1, k1, m1, k6. (15 sts.)
14th row: k7, m1, k1, m1, k7. (17 sts.)
16th row: k8, m1, k1, m1, k8. (19 sts.)
18th row: k9, m1, k1, m1, k9. (21 sts.)
20th row: k10, m1, k1, m1, k10. (23 sts.)
22nd row: k11, m1, k1, m1, k11. (25 sts.)
24th row: k12, m1, k1, m1, k12. (27 sts.)
26th row: k13, m1, k1, m1, k13. (29 sts.)
28th row: k14, m1, k1, m1, k14. (31 sts.)
29th row: purl all sts, then cont in st st without shaping.

Cont in stripe patt: work 4 rows in col A, 4 rows in col B, 4 rows in col A, then 4 rows in col B. Cont in st st and col A until work measures 11 in (28 cm) from cast-on edge, ending after a ws row.

Next row: p all sts.
Next row,: k1, *k2tog; rep from * to end. Break off yarn, and draw through the rem stitches. Pull together tightly, and fasten off.

Sewing together

- Join the hat seam and tail seam. Stitch the tail securely to the base of the hat seam, so that it hangs from the center back of the hat. Weave in all loose ends neatly on the reverse.

Mohawk Hat

This one is for the baby who really likes to break the rules. Although reminiscent of the punk rock hairstyles that were fashionable way back in the Seventies, the choice of color here is quite restrained. But don't let this curb your creativity. Day-Glo colors were all the rage back then so, if you're brave enough, why not give your baby's mohawk a touch of neon pink, green, or orange at the tips?

CHECKLIST

YOU WILL NEED
- pair of size 3 (3.25 mm) needles
- pair of size 6 (4 mm) needles
- 1 (1:1) 2 oz (50 g) ball light worsted knitting yarn in color A (beige)
- 1(1:1) 2 oz (50 g) ball fur-effect (light worsted-weight) knitting yarn in color B (black)
- tape measure
- bodkin

TO FIT SIZES
0–3 months: chest 16 in (41 cm)
3–6 months: chest 18 in (46 cm)
6–12 months: chest 20 in (51 cm)
NOTE: The hat is designed to fit an average sized baby's head

GAUGE
22 stitches and 30 rows to 4 in (10 cm), measured over stockinette stitch, using size 6 (4 mm) needles
NOTE: This hat has a rolled edge

Hat

Using size 3 (3.25 mm) needles and col A, cast on 71 (78:85) sts.
Knit 1 row, then purl 1 row: these two rows form st st.
Work 6 (6:6) further rows in st st.
Work in k1, p1 rib for ¾ in (2 cm), ending with a ws row.
With rs facing, change to size 6 (4 mm) needles, beg with a knit row, cont in st st until work measures 4 (4½: 4¾) in [10 (11:12) cm], measured from start of rib and ending with a ws row.

CROWN SHAPING

With rs facing, begin crown dec as follows:
1st row: k1, *k2tog, k5; rep from * to end.
2nd and every alt row: purl all sts.
3rd row: k1, *k2tog, k4; rep from * to end.
5th row: k1, *k2tog, k3; rep from * to end.
7th row: k1, *k2tog, k2; rep from * to end.
9th row: k1, *k2tog, k1; rep from * to end.
11th row: k1, *k2tog; rep from * to end.
There are now 11 (12:13) sts.
Break off yarn, draw it through the last sts, pull together tightly, and fasten off securely.

Mohawk

Using size 3 (3.25 mm) needles and col B, cast on 58 (62:66) sts.
Work in k1, p1 rib for 3 (3½:4) in [8 (9:10) cm].
Bind off all sts in rib, and fasten off securely.

Sewing together

- Using matching yarn and a bodkin, stitch the hat seam, then weave in all tails of yarn neatly.
- To position and sew the mohawk in place, put the hat on a head-sized bowl or similar object. Pin the ribbed piece along the back seam, beginning at the top of the ribbed band and working up to the crown of the hat, then down the front center, stopping approximately ¾ in (2 cm) short of the ribbing.
- Sew the cast-on edge neatly to the hat. To make sure that the mohawk stands up nicely, it is a good idea to fold a ¾ in (2 cm) hem along the bound-off edge of the mohawk piece, then stitch in place with matching yarn.

Flying Helmet

This colorful and cozy helmet is perfect for protecting coiffures on windy days, as mini aviators loop the loop in their flying machines or, more realistically, take a speedy turn around the park in the stroller. The helmet has a deep ribbed band and ear flaps, so it will fit snugly around the head, keeping out drafts, while the buttoned chin strap makes sure that this rugged piece of headgear stays put if baby experiences any turbulence during the flight. This baby is now ready for takeoff!

CHECKLIST

YOU WILL NEED
- pair of size 3 (3.25 mm) needles
- pair of size 6 (4 mm) needles
- 1 (1:1) 2 oz (50 g) ball light worsted knitting yarn in turquoise blue
- tape measure
- stitch holders
- bodkin
- 1 turquoise blue button

TO FIT SIZES
0–3 months: chest 16 in (41 cm)
3–6 months: chest 18 in (46 cm)
6–12 months: chest 20 in (51 cm)
NOTE: The hat is designed to fit an average sized baby's head

GAUGE
22 stitches and 30 rows to 4 in (10 cm), measured over stockinette stitch, using size 6 (4 mm) needles
NOTE: When "left" or "right" is referred to in the pattern, it is the left or right part of the garment

Flying helmet

FRONT FOLD-UP FLAP

Using size 3 (3.25 mm) needles, cast on 25 (29: 31) sts.

Work in k1, p1 rib for 2¾ (3: 3½) in [7 (8: 9) cm], ending with a rs row.

Break off yarn and place sts on a stitch holder.

LEFT EAR FLAP AND CHIN STRAP

Using size 3 (3.25 mm) needles, cast on 5 sts.

1st row: k1, p1, k1, p1, k1.

2nd row: p1, k1, p1, k1, p1.

Cont in rib until work measures 1½ (2: 2¼) in [4 (5: 6) cm] from cast-on edge, ending with a 2nd row.

EAR FLAP SHAPING

With rs facing, beg inc, working inc sts into rib pattern:

1st row: rib 2, m1, k1, m1, rib 2. (7 sts)

2nd and every alt row: rib all sts.

3rd row: rib 3, m1, k1, m1, rib 3. (9 sts.)

5th row: rib 4, m1, k1, m1, rib 4. (11 sts.)

7th row: rib 5, m1, k1, m1, rib 5. (13 sts.)

9th row (3rd size only): rib 6, m1, k1, m1, rib 6. (15 sts.)

11th row (3rd size only): rib 7, m1, k1, m1, rib 7. There are now 13 (13: 17) sts in total.

Work in rib for a further 1¼ (1¼: 1½) in [3 (3: 4) cm], ending with a ws row. **

Next row: Cast on 10 (11: 10) sts for back section, rib to end.

Cont in rib until work measures 1¼ (1½: 1½) in [3 (4: 4) cm] from cast-on edge, ending with a ws row.

Place sts on a stitch holder.

RIGHT EAR FLAP AND CHIN STRAP

Using size 3 (3.25 mm) needles, cast on 5 sts.

Next row: p1, k1, p1, k1, p1.

Next row: k1, p1, k1, p1, k1.

Next row: p1, k1, p1, k1, p1.

BUTTONHOLE ROW

With rs facing, k1, p1, yrn, p2tog, k1.

Cont in rib until work measures 1½ (2: 2¼) in [4 (5: 6) cm] from cast-on edge, ending with a ws row.

Cont as for left ear flap shaping to **.

Next row: rib all sts to end of row, then cast on 10 (12: 10) sts, and cont in rib until work measures 1¼ (1½: 1½) in [3 (4: 4) cm] from cast-on edge, ending with a ws row.

Joining row: rib across rs of back section and left ear flap, then across ws of front flap (flap turns back to reveal rs when hat is complete), then rib across rs of right ear flap and back section. (71 [78: 85] sts).

Cont in rib until work measures 3 (3½: 4) in [8 (9: 10) cm] from the point where the ear and front flaps were joined, ending with a ws row.

With rs facing, change to size 6 (4 mm) needles and knit next row, then cont in st st for a further ¾ in (2cm), ending with a ws row.

CROWN SHAPING

With rs facing, begin crown dec as follows:

1st row: k1, *k2tog, k5; rep from * to end. (61 [67: 73] sts.)

2nd and every alt row: purl all sts.

3rd row: k1, *k2tog, k4; rep from * to end. (51 [56: 61] sts.)

5th row: k1, *k2tog, k3; rep from * to end. (41 [45: 49] sts.)

7th row: k1, *k2tog, k2; rep from * to end. (31 [34: 37] sts.)

9th row: k1, *k2tog, k1; rep from * to end. (21 [23: 25] sts.)

11th row: k1, *k2tog; rep from * to last 0 (1: 0) st, k 0 (1: 0). (11 [12: 13] sts.)

13th row: as 11th row.

There are now 6 (7: 7) sts.

Change to size 3 (3.25 mm) needles, and work in k1, p1 rib for 10 rows, then bind off all sts. Break off yarn, then draw it through the last st using a bodkin, and fasten off securely.

Sewing together

❀ Using matching yarn and a bodkin, stitch the hat seam, then weave in all loose ends neatly on the reverse.

❀ Sew the button onto the left chin strap, to correspond with the position of the buttonhole on the right one.

Pumpkin Hat

All children (and many adults) like to dress up for Halloween. Wearing this little hat, your baby will be the cutest trick-or-treater on the block. The basic hat shape is simple enough to knit, but it's the green leaf and stalk details that make it special.

CHECKLIST

YOU WILL NEED
- ❀ pair of size 3 (3.25 mm) needles
- ❀ pair of size 6 (4 mm) needles
- ❀ 1 (1:1) 2 oz (50 g) ball light worsted knitting yarn in color A (orange)
- ❀ 1 (1:1) 2 oz (50 g) ball fur-effect (light worsted weight) knitting yarn in color B (green)
- ❀ tape measure
- ❀ stitch holder
- ❀ bodkin

KEY
- ❀ Col A—orange
- ❀ Col B—green

TO FIT SIZES
0–3 months: chest 16 in (41 cm)
3–6 months: chest 18 in (46 cm)
6–12 months: chest 20 in (51 cm)
NOTE: The hat is designed to fit an average sized baby's head

GAUGE
22 stitches and 30 rows to 4 in (10 cm), measured over stockinette stitch, using size 6 (4 mm) needles

Leaves (make 4 alike)

Using size 3 (3.25 mm) needles and col B, cast on 3 (3:3) sts.
1st and every alternate row: purl all sts.
2nd row: k1, m1, k1, m1, k1. (5 sts.)
4th row: k2, m1, k1, m1, k2. (7 sts.)
6th row: k3, m1, k1, m1, k3. (9 sts.)
Cont in st st until work measures 2 in (5 cm) from cast-on edge, ending with a ws row. Break off yarn, and transfer sts to a stitch holder. Rep for the other 3 leaves.

Hat

Using size 3 (3.25 mm) needles and col A, cast on 80 (86:91) sts.
Work in k1, p1 rib for 1½ in (4 cm), ending with a ws row.
Change to size 6 (4 mm) needles.
Next row: k0 (2:1), *k1, m1, k1; rep from * to end. There are now 120 (128:136) sts.
Next row: p all sts.
Next row: *k11 (12:13), p4; rep from * to end.
Next row: *k4, p11 (12:13); rep from * to end.
Repeat last 2 rows until work measures 5 (5½: 6) in [13 (14:15) cm] from cast-on edge, ending with a ws row.

CROWN SHAPING
1st row: k11 (12:13), *k2tog twice; rep from * to end. (104 [112:120] sts.)

2nd row: *p2tog, p11 (12:13); rep from * to end. (96 [104:112] sts.)
3rd row: *k2, k2tog; rep from * to end. (72 [78:84] sts.}
4th row: *p1, p2tog; rep from * to end. (48 [52:56] sts.)
5th row: *k2, k2tog; rep from * to end. (36 [39:42] sts.)
6th row: p to end dec 0 (3:6) sts evenly across. (36 [36:36] sts.)
Change to col B, and join the 4 leaves to the hat.
7th row: with leaves on top of hat, *k1 st of leaf tog with 1 st of hat; rep from * to end so each st of hat is joined to a st of a leaf. (36 [36:36] sts.)
8th row: *p2tog, p1; rep from * to end. (24 [24:24] sts.)
9th row: *k2tog, k1) rep from * to end. (16 [16:16] sts.)
10th row: *p2tog; rep from * to end. (16 [16:16] sts.)

Stalk

Cont in st st on the rem 8 (8:8) sts for 4 in (10 cm). Bind off, then fasten off securely. NOTE: Knit 1 st from a leaf together with 1 st from the hat crown—in effect working 2 stitches together.

Sewing together

❀ Using col A, stitch hat seam. Using col B, stitch stalk seam and secure to top of hat;. Secure all loose ends neatly on the reverse.

Elvis Hat

Just because your career as an Elvis impersonator didn't take off, that's no reason to deny your son or daughter their chance in the spotlight. And this Elvis hat—or should we say wig?—is one of their best chances at getting there. With a lightly padded quiff and convincing sideburns, it looks like the real thing.

CHECKLIST

YOU WILL NEED
- ❁ pair of size 3 (3.25 mm) needles
- ❁ pair of size 6 (4 mm) needles
- ❁ 1 (1:1) 2 oz (50 g) ball light worsted knitting yarn in black
- ❁ tape measure
- ❁ bodkin
- ❁ stitch holder

TO FIT SIZES
0–3 months: chest 16 in (41 cm)
3–6 months: chest 18 in (46 cm)
6–12 months: chest 20 in (51 cm)
NOTE: The hat is designed to fit an average sized baby's head

GAUGE
22 stitches and 30 rows to 4 in (10 cm), measured over stockinette stitch, using size 6 (4 mm) needles

Hat

SIDEBURNS (MAKE 2 ALIKE)
Using size 3 (3.25 mm) needles, cast on 9 (11: 13) sts.
Work in k1, p1 rib for 2 in (5 cm), ending with a ws row. Fasten off, and transfer sts for both sideburns to a stitch holder.

RIBBING
Using size 3 (3.25 mm) needles and a separate length of yarn, cast on 14 (16: 18) sts, then, with rs facing, work across one sideburn. Now cast on 27 (31: 35) sts, and work across the second sideburn with rs facing, then cast on 14 (16: 18) sts. You now have 73 (85: 97) sts.
Cont in k1, p1 rib for 1½ in (4 cm), ending with a ws row.
Change to size 6 (4 mm) needles.
Cont in k1, p1 rib until work measures 4¼ (4¾: 5) in [11 (12: 13) cm] from cast-on edge.

CROWN SHAPING
1st row: k1, *k2tog, k4; rep from * to end.
Next and every alternate row: purl all sts.
3rd row: k1, *k2tog, k3; rep from * to end.
5th row: k1, *k2tog, k2; rep from * to end.
7th row: k1, *k2tog, k1; rep from * to end.
9th row: k1, *k2tog; rep from * to end.
11th row: as 9th row.

There are now 7 (8: 9) sts.
Break off the yarn, leaving a 12 in (30 cm) tail, and draw the yarn through the sts on the needle using a bodkin. Draw up tightly, and fasten off.

QUIFF
Using size 3 (3.25 mm) needles, cast on 28 (32: 36) sts.
Work in k1, p1 rib for 6¼ (7: 8) in [16 (18: 20) cm], ending with a ws row.
Next row: *k2 tog; rep from * to end.
Break off yarn, pass it through the remaining sts using a bodkin, draw up tightly, and fasten off.

Sewing together

- ❁ Join the hat seam.
- ❁ Sew the cast-on edge of the quiff to the cast-on edge at the front of the hat between the sideburns.
- ❁ Stitch the sides of the quiff to the hat for 2¾ (3¼: 3½) in [7 (8: 9) cm] from cast-on edge. Now roll the gathered top edge of the quiff in on itself to form a rounded shape. Secure the roll to the hat with a few stitches on the reverse.
- ❁ Make sure that all loose ends are neatly woven in on the reverse.

Cupcake Hat

Your little cherub will look good enough to eat when wearing this delicious, freshly baked cupcake, complete with a cherry on the top. We've chosen to decorate our cake with classic strawberry-flavored pink frosting, but you could use any color you fancy—such as lemon, pistachio, or lavender or grape—or perhaps embellish the top with sprinkles made from tiny beads or sequins. It's also very easy to imitate colorful chocolate beans by knitting in a few bobbles using the technique described on page 20 and using small scraps of yarn left over from other projects.

CHECKLIST

YOU WILL NEED
- ✿ pair of size 3 (3.25 mm) needles
- ✿ pair of size 6 (4 mm) needles
- ✿ 1 (1:1) 2 oz (50 g) ball light worsted knitting yarn in color A (white)
- ✿ 1 (1:1) 2 oz (50 g) ball light worsted knitting yarn in color B (blue)
- ✿ 1 (1:1) 2 oz (50 g) ball light worsted knitting yarn in color C (brown)
- ✿ 1 (1:1) 2 oz (50 g) ball light worsted knitting yarn in color D (pink)
- ✿ oddment of light worsted knitting yarn in color E (red)
- ✿ tape measure
- ✿ stitch holder
- ✿ bodkin

TO FIT SIZES
0–3 months: chest 16 in (41 cm)
3–6 months: chest 18 in (46 cm)
6–12 months: chest 20 in (51 cm)
NOTE: The hat is designed to fit an average sized baby's head

GAUGE
22 stitches and 30 rows to 4 in (10 cm), measured over stockinette stitch, using size 6 (4 mm) needles

Hat

Using size 6 (4 mm) needles and col A, cast on 72 (78: 87) sts.

Knit 1 row, then purl 1 row. These two rows form st st.

Work 6 (6: 6) more rows st st.

Cont in k2, p1 rib as follows, to form the striped cake case:

*k2 in col A, then p1 in col B; rep from * to end.

Cont in rib until work measures 1¼ (1½: 1½) in [3 (4: 4) cm] from beg of rib.

Change to size 3 (3.25 mm) needles, and cont in rib until work measures 2½ (2¾: 3) in [6 (7: 8) cm] from beg of rib, ending with a ws row.

Cont in rib using col A only for a further 4 rows.

Next row: purl all sts. **

Work in k1, p1 rib for a further 6 rows, dec 1 (0: 2) sts on last row.

Change to size 6 (4 mm) needles and col C, and knit 1 row (baking the cake).

Cont in st st until work measures 3 (3½: 4) in [8 (9: 10) cm], measured from ** and ending with a ws row.

With rs facing, change to col D, and knit 1 row (icing the cake).

Next row: knit all sts.

Cont in rev st st until work measures 4 (4½: 4¾) in [10 (11: 12) cm], measured from single purl row, and ending with a ws row.

CROWN SHAPING

With rs facing, begin crown dec as follows:

1st row: k1, *k2tog, k5; rep from * to end.

Next and every alt row: purl all sts.

3rd row: k1, *k2tog, k4; rep from * to end.

5th row: k1, *k2tog, k3; rep from * to end.

7th row: k1, *k2tog, k2; rep from * to end.

9th row: k1, *k2tog, k1; rep from * to end.

11th row: k1, *k2tog; rep from * to end.

There are now 11 (13: 15) sts remaining.

Break off yarn, and draw it through the last sts using a bodkin, then fasten off securely.

CHERRY

Using size 3 (3.25 mm) needles and col E,
cast on 3 sts.
1st row: k1, m1, k1, m1, k1. (5 sts.)
Next and every alt row: purl all sts.
3rd row: k1, *m1, k1; rep from * to end. (9 sts.)
5th row: k1, *m1, k1; rep from * to end.
There are now 17 sts in total.
Purl 1 row.
Knit 1 row.
Purl 1 row.
Next row: k1, *k2tog; rep from * to end.
Break off yarn, and draw through last 9 sts using
a bodkin, pull together tightly, then fasten off yarn
and join seam. Leave a tail of yarn, so that you
can sew the cherry to the top of the cupcake.

Sewing together

✿ Using matching yarn and a bodkin, stitch the
hat seam and the rib seam, then weave in all tails
neatly on the reverse. Finally, sew the cherry
securely to the top of the cupcake.

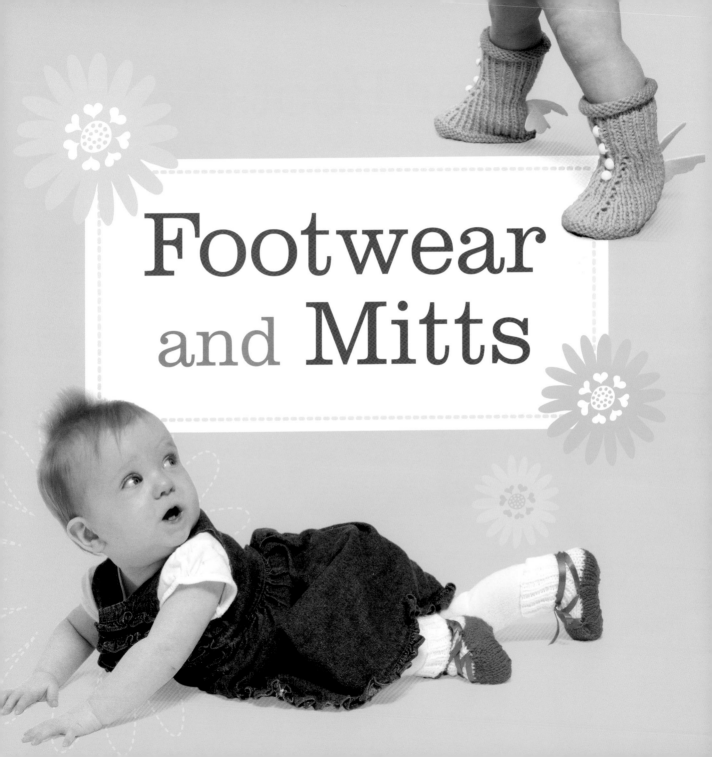

Footwear
and Mitts

Monster Boots and Mitts

The lime green textured yarn used for this boot-and-mitt ensemble looks like funky monster skin when knitted, complete with warts, and all. The cotton mix fibers are very soft and snuggly. And when a job's worth doing, it's worth overdoing … so add a full set of long red monster claws for that perfect finishing touch.

CHECKLIST

YOU WILL NEED

* pair of size 3 (3.25 mm) needles
* pair of size 6 (4 mm) needles
* 2 (2: 2) 2 oz (50 g) balls textured (light worsted-weight) knitting yarn in color A (green)
* oddment of light worsted knitting yarn in color B (red)
* tape measure
* bodkin
* stitch holder

TO FIT SIZES

0–3 months: chest 16 in (41 cm)
3–6 months: chest 18 in (46 cm)
6–12 months: chest 20 in (51 cm)
NOTE: The boots and mitts are designed to fit an average sized baby

GAUGE

22 stitches and 30 rows to 4 in (10 cm), measured over stockinette stitch, using size 6 (4 mm) needles—check gauge first

Monster boots (make 2)

Using size 3 (3.25 mm) needles and col A, cast
on 34 (37:40) sts.
Work in k1, p1 rib for 3 (3½:4) in [8 (9:10) cm],
ending with a ws row.

INSTEP SHAPING

With rs facing, rib 22 (24:26) sts, turn, then rib
10 (11:12) sts, turn, and work on the center
10 (11:12) sts for the instep.
With rs facing, change to size 6 (4 mm) needles,
and knit next 10 (10:12) rows.

Break off yarn, and rejoin to beg of instep. Pick
up and knit 10 (10:12) sts along side of instep,
then work across 10 (11:12) sts at toe.
Now pick up and knit 10 (10:12) sts along other
side of instep, and work across sts on needle.
There should now be 54 (57:64) sts in total.
Knit 13 (15:17) rows.

SOLE DECREASE

With rs facing, *k1, k2tog; rep from * to last 0
(0:1) sts, then k0 (0:1).
Purl 1 row.

Next row: *k1, k2tog; rep from * to last 0 (2:1)
sts, then k0 (2:1).
Bind off all sts in rib, and fasten off securely.

Mitts (make 2)

Using size 3 (3.25 mm) needles and col A, cast
on 22 (24:26) sts.
Work in k1, p1 rib for 1½ in (4 cm), ending with
a ws row.
With rs facing, change to size 6 (4 mm) needles,
and knit 2 (4:6) rows.

THUMB OPENING

With rs facing, k8 (9:10) sts, then slip next 6 sts
onto a stitch holder.
Cast on 4 sts, then work the rem 8 (9:10) sts.
There are now 20 (22:24) sts.
Knit 17 (19:21) rows.

SHAPE TOP OF MITT

With rs facing, k1, k2tog, k4 (5:6), k2tog, k2,
k2tog, k4 (5:6), k2tog, k1.
Bind off all sts, and fasten off securely.

THUMB
Rejoin yarn, and cast on 2 sts, work 6 sts held on stitch holder, then cast on 2 sts. You now have 10 (10: 10) sts.

Knit 8 (8: 10) rows.

SHAPE TOP OF THUMB
Next row: k2tog to end. Thread yarn through rem sts, draw up, and secure.

CLAWS (MAKE 4 LARGE, 12 SMALL)
Using 3 (3.25 mm) needles and col B, cast on 3 sts.

Purl 1 row.

Next row: k1, m1, k1, m1, k1. (5 sts.)

Purl 1 row.

For small claw, work 2 more rows in st st, then bind off.

For large claw, work 6 more rows, then bind off.

Sewing together the monster boots

✿ Join sole and leg seam together, and weave in all loose ends on the reverse.

✿ Fold each claw in half, and join the seam from tip to about halfway toward the bound-off edge. Open out the bound-off edge, and stitch to the toe of the monster boot (using the picture as a guide), with one large claw and three small claws for each boot.

✿ Finally, thread a bodkin with yarn A, make 2 large overstitches between each claw, and pull up tightly to form a small rounded shape on the underside, to accentuate the toes.

Sewing together the monster mitts

✿ Using yarn A, join the thumb and main seams, and weave in all loose ends neatly on the reverse.

✿ Join claw seams as before, and sew one large claw to each thumb, and three small claws to the main part of each mitt.

Pointy Slippers

These cute slippers require very little yarn and are ideal for using up oddments left over from other garments, so that baby can have shoes to match the outfit. You could even knit the main part of each slipper in multicolored stripes, with a contrasting cuff, or vice versa. Finish the slippers with pretty ribbon bows in a matching or contrasting color.

CHECKLIST

YOU WILL NEED
- 🌸 pair of size 3 (3.25 mm) needles
- 🌸 pair of size 6 (4 mm) needles
- 🌸 1(1:1) 2 oz (50 g) ball light worsted knitting yarn in yellow
- 🌸 4 ft (1.22 m) of ⅛ in (5 mm) wide ribbon
- 🌸 stitch holder
- 🌸 tape measure
- 🌸 bodkin

TO FIT SIZES
0–3 months: chest 16 in (41 cm)
3–6 months: chest 18 in (46 cm)
6–12 months: chest 20 in (51 cm)
NOTE: The slippers are designed to fit an average sized baby

GAUGE
22 stitches and 30 rows to 4 in (10 cm), measured over stockinette stitch, using size 6 (4 mm) needles
NOTE: The actual weight of the finished pair of slippers is 1 oz (25 g)—you can use this weight to calculate how much yarn you will need if using leftovers from other projects

SPECIAL ABBREVIATIONS
(see page 19 for standard abbreviations)
m1—increase one stitch by picking up and knitting the loop that lies between stitches, making a decorative hole (see page 18).

Slippers (make 2 alike)

Using size 6 (4 mm) needles, cast on 6 sts.
1st row and every alt row: purl all sts.
2nd row: k1, m1, k4, m1, k1.
4th row: k2, m1, k4, m1, k2.
6th row: k3, m1, k4, m1, k3.
8th row: k4, m1, k4, m1, k4.
10th row: k5, m1, k4, m1, k5.
Cont increasing 1 st on either side of the center 4 sts until you have 28 (30: 32) sts.
Purl 1 row.

DIVIDE FOR ANKLE OPENING

With rs facing, knit 14 (15: 16) sts, turn, and transfer rem sts to a stitch holder.

SHAPE HEEL

With rs facing, bind off 3 (3: 4) sts.
Cont in st st for a further 9 (9: 11) rows.
With rs facing, bind off 3 (3: 4) sts.
Cont in st st for 4 (4: 5) rows, then bind off all sts.
Rejoin yarn to sts held on the stitch holder; then work the second side to match, reversing the shapings accordingly.

CUFF

With rs facing, using size 3 (3.25 mm) needles, pick up and knit 15 (15: 18) sts evenly from the back of the ankle to the center of the instep, then pick up and knit 15(15: 18) sts evenly from the center of the instep to the back of the ankle.
Next row (1st and 2nd sizes only): work in p1, k1 rib for 14 sts, p2, then k1, p1 to end.
Next row (3rd size only): work in k1, p1 rib for 17 sts, p2, then k1, p1 to end.
Work another 2 rows in this way for each size.

DIVIDE CUFF

With rs facing, rib 15 (15: 18) sts, turn, and transfer rem sts to stitch holder.
Cont in rib until work measures 2 in (5 cm) from beg of rib, ending with a ws row.
Bind off all sts in rib, and fasten off securely.
Work the other half of the cuff in the same way.

Sewing together

🌸 Join sole and leg seam together, and weave in all loose ends on the reverse.

🌸 Cut the ribbon in half, and thread one piece through each of the slippers in a crisscross pattern over the instep, using the picture as a guide. Tie the ribbons at the ankles in pretty bows.

Furry Bear Feet

No fashion-forward baby should be seen this season without these furry boots, which are warm, stretchy, and comfortable. Fur-effect yarn knits up quickly and produces a soft, thick fabric that looks authentic. Hand-stitch some felt "pads" to the sole of each boot, using the templates provided on page 105, to complete the furry bear effect.

CHECKLIST

YOU WILL NEED
❋ pair of size 3 (3.25 mm) needles
❋ 1(1:1) 2 oz (50 g) ball fur-effect (light worsted-weight) knitting yarn in brown
❋ 9 in (23 cm) square of beige felt
❋ 9 in (23 cm) square of brown felt
❋ tracing paper
❋ tape measure
❋ bodkin
❋ fabric adhesive
❋ sewing needle
❋ matching thread

TO FIT SIZES
0–3 months: chest 16 in (41 cm)
3–6 months: chest 18 in (46 cm)
6–12 months: chest 20 in (51 cm)
NOTE: The boots are designed to fit an average sized baby

GAUGE
22 stitches and 30 rows to 4 in (10 cm), measured over stockinette stitch, using size 6 (4 mm) needles
NOTE: Size 3 (3.25 mm) needles and k1, p1 rib used throughout

Bear feet (make 2 alike)

Using size 3 (3.25 mm) needles, cast on 27 (31:35) sts.

Work in k1, p1 rib for 3 in (8 cm), ending with a ws row.

Next row: rib 17 (20:23) sts, turn, and rib 7 (9:11) sts.

Work 8 (10:12) rows in rib on these rem 7 (9:11) sts.

INSTEP SHAPING

With rs facing, break off yarn and rejoin to beg of instep. Pick up and knit 8 (10:12) sts along side of instep, then work across 7 (9:11) sts at toe.

Now pick up and knit 8 (10:12) sts along other side of instep, and work across sts on needle. There are now 43 (51:59) sts in total.

Work in k1, p1 rib for 7 (9:9) rows.

SOLE DECREASE

With rs facing, *k1, k2tog; rep from * to last 1 (0:2) sts, then k to end.

There are now 29 (34:40) sts.

Purl 1 row.

Next row: *k1, k2tog; rep from * to last 2 (1:1) sts, then k to end.

There are now 20 (23:27) sts.

Purl 1 row.

Bind off all sts in rib, and fasten off securely.

Sewing together

❋ Join sole and leg seam together, and weave in all loose ends on the reverse.

❋ Trace off the sole template from page 105 onto tracing paper, and cut out.

❋ Use the templates to cut two soles in beige felt and two sets of pads in brown felt.
NOTE: Remember to reverse the template, so that you have a right foot and a left foot.

❋ Use fabric adhesive to glue the pads to the soles. Pin the soles to the underside of the bear feet and, using matching sewing thread, blanket stitch securely into position.

Ballerina Socks

These incredibly cute ballerina socks will keep tiny toes warm and pretty. Shiny pink satin ribbons are crisscrossed softly around the ankle and tied in a bow, so that baby can't lose them while practicing those high kicks when out in the stroller or relaxing in the crib. Even so, it might be useful to knit a spare pair—just in case.

CHECKLIST

YOU WILL NEED
✿ pair of size 3 (3.25 mm) needles
✿ pair of size 6 (4 mm) needles
✿ 1(1:1) 2 oz (50 g) ball light worsted knitting yarn in color A (white)
✿ 1(1:1) 2 oz (50 g) ball light worsted knitting yarn in color B (pink)
✿ 2½ yds (2.3 m) of ¼ in (6 mm) wide pink satin ribbon
✿ bodkin

TO FIT SIZES
0–3 months: chest 16 in (41 cm)
3–6 months: chest 18 in (46 cm)
6–12 months: chest 20 in (51 cm)
NOTE: The socks are designed to fit an average sized baby

GAUGE
22 stitches and 30 rows to 4 in (10 cm), measured over stockinette stitch, using size 6 (4 mm) needles
NOTE: The actual weight of the finished pair of socks is 1 oz (25 g)—you can use this weight to calculate how much yarn you will need if using leftovers from other projects

Ballerina socks (make 2 alike)

Using size 3 (3.25 mm) needles and col A, cast on 27 (31:35) sts.
Work in k1, p1 rib for 3 in (8 cm), ending with a ws row.
Next row: rib 17 (20:23) sts, turn, rib 7 (9:11) sts.
With rs facing, work 6 (6:8) rows in rib on the rem 7 (9:11) sts.
Change to size 6 (4 mm) needles and col B, and cont in st st for 2 (4:4) more rows.

INSTEP SHAPING
With rs facing, break off yarn, and rejoin col B to beg of instep. Pick up and knit 8 (10:12) sts along side of instep, then work across 7 (9:11) sts at toe.
Now pick up and knit 8 (10:12) sts along other side of instep, then work across sts on needle.
There are now 43 (51:59) sts in total.
Work in st st for 7 (9:9) rows.

SOLE DECREASE
With rs facing, *k1, k2tog); rep from * to last 1 (0:2) sts, then k to end.
There are now 29 (34:40) sts.
Purl 1 row.
Next row: *k1, k2tog; repeat from * to last 2 (1:1) sts, then k to end.
There are now 20 (23:27) sts.
Purl 1 row.
Bind off all sts in rib, and fasten off securely.

Sewing together
✿ Use matching colored yarns to join sole and leg seams.
✿ Cut the length of ribbon in half, and thread one piece through each of the socks in a crisscross pattern over the insteps, using the picture as a guide. The ribbons can be tied around the baby's ankles in pretty bows.

Winged Booties

Winged footwear seems to have been a fashionable accessory in Greek and Roman mythology. Hermes and Mercury were messengers for the gods and were required to make speedy airmail deliveries, hence the wings. The wings on these baby boots are for decorative purposes only, however, and do not facilitate flight.

CHECKLIST

YOU WILL NEED
- pair of size 3 (3.25 mm) needles
- 1 (1: 1) 2 oz (50 g) ball light worsted knitting yarn in color A (blue)
- 1 (1: 1) 2 oz (50 g) ball light worsted knitting yarn in color B (pink)
- 9 in (23 cm) square of white felt
- 8 white buttons
- tape measure
- bodkin
- tracing paper
- sewing needle
- white sewing thread

TO FIT SIZES
0–3 months: chest 16 in (41 cm)
3–6 months: chest 18 in (46 cm)
6–12 months: chest 20 in (51 cm)
NOTE: The boots are designed to fit an average sized baby

GAUGE
22 stitches and 30 rows to 4 in (10 cm), measured over stockinette stitch, using size 6 (4 mm) needles.
NOTE: The largest pair of boots weighs 1¼ oz (35 g)—use this weight to calculate yarn amounts

SPECIAL ABBREVIATIONS
(see page 19 for standard abbreviations)
m1—increase one stitch by picking up and knitting the loop that lies between stitches, making a decorative hole.

Winged boots (make 2 alike)

Using size 3 (3.25 mm) needles and col A, cast on 31 (33: 35) sts.
Knit 1 row.
Purl 1 row.
Cont in st st for a further 6 rows.
With rs facing, change to col B, and knit 1 row.
Work in k1, p1 rib for 1¼ (1½: 2) in [3 (4: 5) cm], ending with a ws row.
With rs facing, begin instep shaping as follows:
1st row: rib 13 (14: 15) sts, m1, rib 5 sts, m1, rib to end.
Next and every alt row: rib all sts, taking extra sts into rib pattern as set.
3rd row: rib 14 (15: 16) sts, m1, rib 5 sts, m1, rib to end.
5th row: rib 15 (16: 17) sts, m1, rib 5 sts, m1, rib to end.
Cont increasing 1 st on either side of the center 5 sts until you have 51 (53: 55) sts.

Work 3 rows in rib.
Next row: with rs facing, change to col A, and knit 2 rows.
Cont in reverse st st for 4 rows.
With rs facing, begin sole dec as follows:
*k1, k2tog; rep from * to last 0 (2: 1) sts, then k0 (2: 1) sts. You should now have 34 (36: 37) sts.
Next row: purl.
Next row: knit.
Next row: purl.
Bind off all sts in rib, and fasten off securely.

Sewing together

- Using matching yarns, join sole and leg seams together, and weave in all loose ends on the reverse.
- Trace off the wings template from page 105 onto tracing paper. Use to cut out two pairs of wings from white felt.
- Crease along the center line of each pair, and stitch the fold securely to the back of the heel of each boot.
- Sew four buttons to the front of each boot.

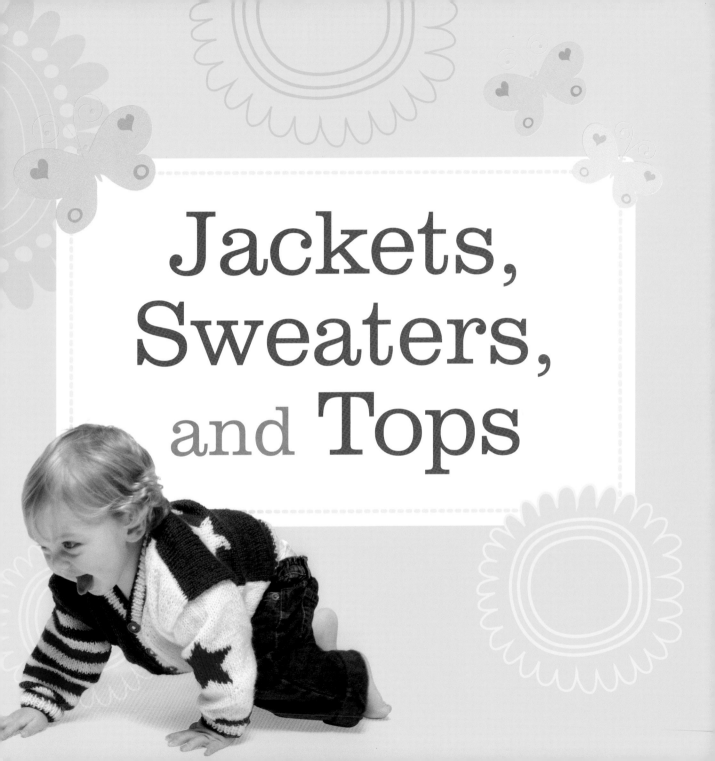

Jackets, Sweaters, and Tops

Red Riding Hood

Practical and striking, this full-length garment doubles as a sleeping bag for babies on the move. The design is generously sized, so that the garment will fit over light underclothes and not restrict movement. Babies come in all sizes, as we know, so be sure to measure the length of your baby before you begin knitting. You can alter the length of the pattern, so that she can stretch out when the lower flap is buttoned.

CHECKLIST

YOU WILL NEED
- pair of size 3 (3.25 mm) needles
- pair of size 6 (4 mm) needles
- size 3 (3.25 mm) circular needle
- 6 (7:8) 2 oz (50 g) balls light worsted knitting yarn in color red
- 4 red buttons
- tape measure
- stitch holders
- bodkin

TO FIT SIZES
0–3 months: chest 16 in (41 cm)
3–6 months: chest 18 in (46 cm)
6–12 months: chest 20 in (51 cm)

GAUGE
22 stitches and 30 rows to 4 in (10 cm), measured over stockinette stitch, using size 6 (4 mm) needles

Back

Using size 3 (3.25 mm) needles, cast on 53 (59:65) sts.
Beg with a knit row, then cont for 7 more rows in st st.
Work in k1, p1 rib for 4 rows.

BUTTONHOLE ROW

Rib 6 sts, * bind off 2 sts, rib 11 (13:15) sts; rep from * to last 8 sts, bind off 2 sts, rib to end.
Next row: work in k1, p1 rib, casting on 2 sts over each buttonhole.
Cont in rib for 4 more rows.
With rs facing, change to size 6 (4 mm) needles, and cont in st st until work measures 25½ (27:28½) in [65 (69:73) cm] from beg of rib, ending with a ws row.

SHOULDER SHAPING

With rs facing, bind off 8 (9:10) sts at beg of next 2 rows, then 9 (10:11) sts at beg of foll 2 rows.
Slip rem 19 (21:23) sts onto a stitch holder for back neck.

Front

Using size 3 (3.25 mm) needles, cast on 53 (59:65) sts.
Work in k1, p1 rib for 1¼ in (3 cm), ending with a ws row.
Change to size 6 (4 mm) needles, and cont in st st until work measures 17½ (19:20½) in [44 (48:52) cm] from cast-on edge, ending with a ws row.

DIVIDE FOR FRONT OPENING

With rs facing, work 24 (27:30) sts, turn, and cont on these sts for left front.
Slip rem sts onto a stitch holder for right front.
Cont without shaping until work measures 19½ (21:22½) in [49 (53:57) cm] from cast-on edge, ending with a rs row.

NECKLINE SHAPING

With ws facing, bind off 2 (3:4) sts, then work to end.

Dec 1 st at end and at same edge of next 5 (5:5) rows.

Cont without shaping until work measures 21 (22½:24) in [53 (57:61) cm] from cast-on edge, ending with a ws row.

SHOULDER SHAPING

Bind off 8 (9:10) sts at beg of next row, work 1 row, then bind off rem 9 (10:11) sts, and fasten off securely.

Rejoin yarn to the sts on stitch holder. Bind off the first 5 sts at center front, then cont on rem sts for right front, following neckline and shoulder shaping as before, but reversing shapings to make corresponding right front.

> **PATTERN (FOR SLEEVE)**
> 1st row: knit.
> 2nd row: purl.
> 3rd row: knit.
> 4th row: purl.
> 5th row: knit.
> 6th row: knit.
> These 6 rows form the pattern.
> *NOTE: This design has a rolled edge on the button flap and hood*

Sleeve (make 2 alike)

Using size 3 (3.25 mm) needles, cast on 33 (35: 37) sts.

Work in k1, p1 rib for 1¼ in (3 cm), ending with a ws row.

Change to size 6 (4 mm) needles, and cont in the sleeve pattern (see box, above), increasing as follows:

Inc 1 st at both ends of next and every foll 4th row until there are 45 (49: 53) sts.

Cont without shaping until work measures 6 (6½: 8) in [15 (17: 20) cm] from cast-on edge, ending with a ws row.

ARMHOLE SHAPING

With rs facing, bind off 9 (10 : 11) sts at beg of next 4 rows. Bind off rem 9 sts, and fasten off securely.

Hood

First join the shoulder seams.

With rs facing and using size 6 (4 mm) needles, pick up and knit 18 (20: 22) sts evenly up right front neck.

Knit 19 (21: 23) sts held on stitch holder for back neck, then pick up and knit 18 (20: 22) sts evenly down left front neck.

Next row: purl.

Inc row: work 18 (20: 22) sts, m1 st between each of next 19 (21: 23) sts, then work to end.

Cont in st st until hood measures 8 (9: 10) in [20 (22: 25) cm], then bind off all sts, and fasten off securely.

Using a bodkin and col A, join hood seam.

BAND

Using size 3 (3.25 mm) circular needle, pick up and knit 12 (12: 12) sts along right front opening to neck, then 46 (52: 58) sts along right side of hood to seam, 46 (52: 58) sts to neck, and 12 (12: 12) sts along left front opening.

Work in k1, p1 rib for 1¼ in (3 cm), ending with a ws row.

Next row: knit all sts.

Cont in st st for 5 more rows, then bind off all sts in rib, and fasten off securely.

Sewing together

❀ Using a bodkin, join both shoulder seams. Measure 4¼ (4¾: 5¼) in [11 (12: 13) cm] down each side edge from the shoulder seam, and mark with pins.

❀ Stitch the armhole edge of each sleeve in position between the marked points.

❀ Join side and sleeve seams.

❀ Overlap the bands at the center front, and sew the lower edges to the bound-off edge at the center front opening.

❀ Weave in all loose ends on the reverse.

❀ Sew four buttons onto the front, to correspond with the buttonholes in the flap.

Ballet Top with Tulle Tutu

This stretchy ribbed sweater has a tulle tutu and ribbon bows stitched to its hem.
When baby doesn't want to be a ballerina anymore, you can easily remove them.

CHECKLIST

YOU WILL NEED
- pair of size 3 (3.25 mm) needles
- pair of size 6 (4 mm) needles
- 3 (3:3) 2 oz (50 g) balls light worsted knitting yarn in color A (pink)
- 4 pink buttons
- 2¼ yds (2 m) of 1 in (25 mm) wide pink satin ribbon
- 24 in (60 cm) of 56 in (140 cm) wide pink tulle or other net fabric
- 20 in (50 cm) of ⅜ in (1 cm) wide elastic
- tape measure
- stitch holders
- bodkin
- large safety pin

TO FIT SIZES
0–3 months: chest 16 in (41 cm)
3–6 months: chest 18 in (46 cm)
6–12 months: chest 20 in (51 cm)

GAUGE
22 stitches and 30 rows to 4 in (10 cm), measured over stockinette stitch, using size 6 (4 mm) needles
NOTE: Ballet top worked in k1, p1 rib throughout

Ballet top

BACK
Using size 3 (3.25 mm) needles, cast on 53 (59:65) sts.
Work in k1, p1 rib for 1¼ in (3 cm), ending with a ws row.
Change to size 6 (4 mm) needles, and cont in rib until work measures 7½ (9: 10½) in [19 (23:27) cm] from cast-on edge, ending with a ws row.

SHOULDER SHAPING
With rs facing, bind off 8 (9: 10) sts at beg of next 2 rows, then 9 (10: 11) sts at beg of foll 2 rows.
Slip rem 19 (21:23) sts onto a stitch holder for back neck.

LEFT FRONT
Using size 3 (3.25 mm) needles, cast on 53 (59:65) sts.
Work in k1, p1 rib for 1¼ in (3 cm), ending with a ws row.
Change to size 6 (4 mm) needles, and cont in rib until work measures 3 (4½:5½) in [8 (11:14) cm] from cast-on edge, ending with a ws row.

DIVIDE FOR LEFT FRONT OPENING
With rs facing, rib 24 (27:30) sts, then cast on 5 sts for button band. (29 [32:35] sts.)
Cont in rib on these stitches only until work measures 5½ (7:8½) in [14 (18:22) cm] from cast-on edge, ending with a ws row.

NECKLINE SHAPING
With rs facing, rib 22 (24:26) sts, turn, then place rem 7 (8:9) sts on a stitch holder for front neck.
Dec 1 st at beg of next row, and at same end of next 4 rows. (17 [19:21] sts.)
Cont in rib without shaping until work measures 7½ (9: 10½) in [19 (23:27) cm], ending with a ws row.

SHOULDER SHAPING
With rs facing, bind off 8 (9: 10) sts at beg of next row. Work 1 row, then bind off rem 9 (10: 11) sts, and fasten off securely.

RIGHT FRONT

With rs facing, rejoin yarn to rem 29 (32:35) sts, then cont in rib as follows:

Work 2 (2:4) rows in rib.

Buttonhole row: With rs facing, rib 2, yrn, p2 tog, rib to end*.

Rib 5 (7:7) rows, then rep buttonhole row*.

Rep from * to * once, then work buttonhole row again.

Cont in rib until work measures 5½ (7:8½) in [14 (18:22) cm] from cast-on edge, ending with a rs row.

Now cont in rib, following neckline and shoulder shaping as before, reversing shapings to make corresponding right front.

SLEEVE (MAKE 2)

Using size 3 (3.25 mm) needles cast on 33 (35:37) sts.

Work in k1, p1 rib for 1¼ in (3 cm), ending with a ws row.

Change to size 6 (4 mm) needles, and cont in rib.

SLEEVE SHAPING

Inc 1 st at both ends of next and every foll 4th row until there are 45 (49:53) sts.

Cont without shaping until work measures 6 (6½:8) in [15 (17:20) cm] from cast-on edge, ending with a ws row.

ARMHOLE SHAPING

With rs facing, bind off 9 (10:11) sts at beg of next 4 rows.

Bind off rem 9 sts, and fasten off securely.

NECKBAND

First join the shoulder seams.

NOTE Use a circular needle to do this if you find it easier.

Using size 3 (3.25 mm) needles, and with rs facing, rib sts from right front neck, then pick up and knit 14 (14:14) sts evenly around neckline

to shoulder; rib 19 (21:23) sts from back neck, pick up and knit 14 (14:14) sts evenly around left front neck to center front, then rib sts from left front neck.

Work 3 rows in rib.

BUTTONHOLE ROW

With rs facing, rib 2 sts , yrn, p2tog, rib to end. Work a further 3 rows in rib, then bind off all sts in rib, and fasten off securely.

Sewing together

✿ Measure 4¼ (4¾: 5¼) in [11(12:13) cm] down each side edge from the shoulder seam, then mark the position with pins. Stitch the armhole edge of each sleeve into position between the marked points.

✿ Join side and sleeve seams.

✿ Overlap front opening at lower edges, and sew cast-on edge in place.

✿ Weave in all loose ends on the wrong side.

✿ Sew four buttons onto the left front button band, to correspond with buttonholes on the right front.

Tulle tutu

✿ Cut two 12 x 56 in (30 x 140 cm) strips from the pink tulle. Fold each in half widthwise and, using a ⅝ in (1.5 cm) seam allowance, machine-sew the short sides together to make two tubes. Place the tubes one inside the other with reverse sides facing. Now fold the tubes of tulle in half, matching the long edges, to make a four-layer tube with a fold at the upper edge and the raw edges at the lower edge. Machine-sew a casing approximately ¾ in (2 cm) from the top fold.

✿ Snip a few stitches in one seam in the casing, and use a large safety pin to thread the elastic through. Adjust the elastic to fit the child's waist, then stitch the ends together securely.

✿ Hand-stitch the casing to the wrong side of the rib at the hem. Stretch the elastic as you go, so that it will stretch with the knitted garment when it is worn.

✿ Cut the ribbon into four equal lengths, and tie each one into a bow. Stitch two to the front and two to the back of the top, where it meets the tulle tutu.

Tiny Biker Jacket

Oh yes, this baby was definitely born to be wild and is looking for adventure. Any baby will look super cool in this classic biker-style jacket complete with chunky zipper front opening and wing motif on the back yoke. We chose black for our jacket, but the design would work equally well in any color that takes your fancy, so why not try hot pink or bright red instead? Add more embroidered patches to the sleeves, or perhaps a row of shiny buttons, to imitate metal studs for that authentic biker look.

CHECKLIST

YOU WILL NEED
- pair of size 3 (3.25 mm) needles
- pair of size 6 (4 mm) needles
- 3 (4:4) 2 oz (50 g) balls light worsted knitting yarn in black
- black open-ended zipper, 7 (8: 10) in (18 [20: 25] cm) long
- wing patch
- star patches
- tape measure
- stitch holder
- bodkin
- sewing needle and thread

TO FIT SIZES
0–3 months: chest 16 in (41 cm)
3–6 months: chest 18 in (46 cm)
6–12 months: chest 20 in (51 cm)

GAUGE
22 stitches and 30 rows to 4 in (10 cm), measured over stockinette stitch, using size 6 (4 mm) needles

NOTE: The biker jacket is knitted in stockinette stitch with ribbed side panels, yoke, and collar. The overlap and underlap have facings, and the left front is made in two pieces to facilitate insertion of the zipper.

Back
Using size 3 (3.25 mm) needles, cast on 53 (59:65) sts.
Work in k1, p1 rib (1st and 3rd sizes), and p1, k1 rib (2nd size) for 1¼ in (3 cm), ending with a ws row.
Change to size 6 (4 mm) needles.

RIB PATTERN (FOR RIBBED SIDE PANEL)
Next row: work in rib for 14 (15: 16) sts, knit to last 14 (15:16) sts, then work in rib to end.
Cont in rib and st st patt as set until work measures 6¼ (7:8) in [16 (18:20) cm] from cast-on edge, ending with a ws row.

RIBBED BACK YOKE
With rs facing, cont in rib until work measures 9 (10¾: 12) in [23 (27: 31) cm] from cast-on edge, ending with a ws row.

SHOULDER SHAPING
With rs facing, bind off 8 (9: 10) sts at beg of next 2 rows, then 9 (10: 11) sts at beg of foll 2 rows.

Slip rem 19 (21:23) sts onto a stitch holder for back neck.

BIKER RIGHT FRONT OVERLAP

Using size 3 (3.25 mm) needles cast on 39 (44:49) sts.

Work in k1, p1 rib for 1¼ in (3 cm), ending with a rs row.

Change to size 6 (4 mm) needles.

RIB PATTERN (FOR RIBBED SIDE PANEL)

Next row: work in k1, p1 rib for 14 (15:16) sts, then purl to end.

Cont in patt until work measures 7½ (9:10½) in [19 (23:27) cm] from cast-on edge, ending with a ws row.

NECK SHAPING

With rs facing, bind off first 17 (20:23) sts. Cont on rem sts for right front neck.

Dec 1 st at end of next and at same edge of foll 4 rows. (17 [19:21] sts.)

Cont without shaping until work measures 9 (10¾:12) in [23 (27:31) cm] from cast-on edge, ending with a rs row.

SHOULDER SHAPING

With ws facing, bind off 8 (9:10) sts at beg of next row. Work 1 row, then bind off rem 9 (10:11) sts, and fasten off securely.

RIGHT FRONT FACING

Using size 6 (4 mm) needles, cast on 25 (29:33) sts.

Cont in st st until work measures 6 (7½:9) in [15 (19:23) cm] from cast-on edge, ending with a rs row.

NECK SHAPING

With ws facing, bind off first 17 (20:23) sts. Cont on rem sts to make right front facing.

Dec 1 st at end of next and at same edge of foll 4 rows. (3 [4:5] sts.)

Cont without shaping until work matches front measured from top of rib to shoulder, ending with a ws row.

Bind off all sts, and fasten off securely.

Left front underlap

RIBBED SIDE SECTION

Using size 3 (3.25 mm) needles, cast on 14 (15:16) sts.

Work in k1, p1 rib (1st and 3rd sizes) and p1, k1 rib (2nd size) for 1¼ in (3 cm), ending with a rs row.

Change to size 6 (4 mm) needles.

Cont in rib until work measures 9 (10¾:12) in [23 (27:31) cm] from cast-on edge, ending with a ws row.

SHOULDER SHAPING

With rs facing, bind off 8 (9:10) sts at beg of next row.

Work 1 row.

Bind off rem sts, and fasten off securely.

CENTER SECTION

Using size 3 (3.25 mm) needles, cast on 25 (29:33) sts.

Work in k1, p1 rib for 1¼ in (3 cm), ending with a ws row.

Change to size 6 (4 mm) needles, and cont in st st until work measures 7½ (9:10½) in [19 (23:27) cm] from cast-on edge, ending with a rs row.

NECK SHAPING

With ws facing, bind off first 17 (20:23) sts. Cont on rem sts for left front neck.

With rs facing, dec 1 st at end of next and at same edge of foll 4 rows. (3 [4:5] sts.)

Cont without shaping until work measures 9 (10¾:12) in [23 (27:31) cm] from cast-on edge, ending with a ws row.

Bind off all sts, and fasten off securely.

LEFT FRONT FACING

Work as for right front facing, but with the shapings reversed.

Sleeve (make 2)

Using size 3 (3.25 mm) needles, cast on 33 (35:37) sts.

Work in k1, p1 rib for 1¼ in (3 cm), ending with a ws row.

Change to size 6 (4 mm) needles, and cont in st st.

Inc 1 st at both ends of next and every foll 4th row until you have 45 (49:53) sts.

Cont without shaping until work measures 6 (6½:8) in [15 (17:20) cm] from cast-on edge, ending with a ws row.

ARMHOLE SHAPING

With rs facing, bind off 9 (10:11) sts at beg of next 4 rows.

Bind off rem 9 sts, and fasten off securely.

Zipper insertion

✿ Place ribbed side section and center section right sides up on your work surface.

✿ Separate the zipper, and place the tape of the right-hand piece under the edge of the ribbed side section. Hand-stitch the knitted edge neatly to the zipper tape.

✿ Now flip the center section over so that it lies right sides together on the ribbed section, matching the edges at shoulder and ribbing. Stitch through all the layers, so that the zipper tape is sandwiched between the ribbed section and the center section. Stitch the other half of the zipper to the center edge of the overlap.

Sewing together and collar

✿ Using a bodkin and col A, join both shoulder seams.

COLLAR

With rs facing, using size 3 (3.25 mm) needles, pick up and knit 20 (21:22) sts evenly around right front neck, beg at end of bound-off sts, then rib 19 (21:23) sts held on stitch holder for back neck, then pick up and knit 20 (21:22) sts down left front neck, ending at beg of bound-off sts at front neck.

Work in k1, p1 rib for 3¼ in (18 cm).

Bind off all sts in rib, and fasten off securely.

✿ Stitch facings to overlap and underlap.

✿ Measure 4¼ (4¾:5¼) in [11 (12:13) cm] down each side edge from the shoulder seam, then mark with pins.

✿ Stitch the armhole edge of each sleeve in position between the marked points.

✿ Join side and sleeve seams.

✿ Weave in all loose ends on the reverse.

✿ Sew wing patches and two star patches to back yoke and three star patches to each sleeve.

Baseball Jacket

This classic preppy jacket in soft colors is great over little jeans or a sleeper for that all-American look. We've used simple stripes on one sleeve and a star motif on the other to add interest, but you could use initials or another motif of your choice.

CHECKLIST

YOU WILL NEED
- pair of size 3 (3.25 mm) needles
- pair of size 6 (4 mm) needles
- size 3 (3.25 mm) circular needle
- 1 (1:1) 2 oz (50 g) ball light worsted knitting yarn in color A (red)
- 1 (1:1) 2 oz (50 g) ball light worsted knitting yarn in color B (blue)
- 1 (1:1) 2 oz (50 g) ball light worsted knitting yarn in color C (cream)
- 4 (4:5) red buttons
- tape measure
- stitch holder
- bodkin

TO FIT SIZES
0–3 months: chest 16 in (41 cm)
3–6 months: chest 18 in (46 cm)
6–12 months: chest 20 in (51 cm)

GAUGE
22 stitches and 30 rows to 4 in (10 cm), measured over stockinette stitch, using size 6 (4 mm) needles

Back
Using size 3 (3.25 mm) needles and col B, cast on 53 (59:65) sts.
Work 1 row in k1, p1 rib. Cont in rib and work 6 rows in col C, 2 rows in col A.
Change to size 6 (4 mm) needles and cont in st st in B until work measures 9 (10½: 12) in [23 (27: 31) cm] from cast-on edge, ending with a ws row.
NOTE If using the intarsia method (see page 21) for the star motifs, follow the chart on page 107. If using duplicate stitch (page 21), cont working the back following the instructions, adding the stars by hand after the knitted piece is complete, using the chart as a guide for positioning.

SHOULDER SHAPING
With rs facing, bind off 8 (9: 10) sts at beg of next 2 rows, then 9 (10: 11) sts at beg of foll 2 rows. Slip rem 19 (21:23) sts onto a stitch holder for back neck.

Left front
Using size 3 (3.25 mm) needles and col B, cast on 24 (27:30) sts.
Work 1 row in k1, p1 rib. Cont in rib, and work 6 rows in col C, 2 rows in col A.
Change to size 6 (4 mm) needles and col C,

and cont in st st until work measures 5½ (6½: 8) in [14 (16: 20) cm] from cast-on edge, ending with a ws row.

NECKLINE SHAPING
With rs facing, dec 1 st at end of next and every foll 4th (4th: 4th) row until 17 (19: 21) sts rem. Cont without shaping until work measures 9 (10½: 12) in [23 (27: 31) cm] from cast-on edge, ending with a ws row.

SHOULDER SHAPING
With rs facing, bind off 8 (9: 10) sts at beg of next row. Work 1 row, then bind off rem 9 (10: 11) sts.

Right front

Work as for left front, but change to col B after ribbed band.
NOTE Reverse shapings to make corresponding right front.

Striped sleeve

Using size 3 (3.25 mm) needles and col B, cast on 33 (35:37) sts.
Work 1 row in k1, p1 rib. Cont in rib, and work 6 rows in col C, then 2 rows in col A.
Change to size 6 (4 mm) needles, and cont in st st and stripe pattern, as follows.

SLEEVE SHAPING

Work 4 rows in col C, 4 rows in col B, 4 rows in col C and 4 rows in col A, at the same time inc 1 st at both ends of next and every foll 4th row until there are 45 (49:53) sts.
Cont without shaping until work measures 6 (6½:8) in [15 (17:20) cm] from cast-on edge, ending with a ws row.

ARMHOLE SHAPING

With rs facing, bind off 9 (10:11) sts at beg of next 4 rows.
Bind off rem 9 sts, and fasten off securely.

Motif sleeve

Work as for striped sleeve, but cont in col C after rib.
Use the pattern chart given on page 106 for positioning of star motif worked in A.
NOTE Remember that you can use either the intarsia method or the duplicate stitch method for working the motifs.

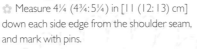

Front band

Join both shoulder seams. With rs facing, using a size 3 (3.25 mm) circular needle and col A, pick up and knit 58 (70: 82) sts evenly along the edge from the lower right center front to the shoulder seam, then knit 19 (21: 23) sts held on stitch holder for back neck, then pick up and k 58 (70: 82) sts from shoulder to lower left center front.

Work 1 row in k1, p1 rib, then change to col C and work 3 rows in rib.

Buttonhole row: With ws facing, work 4 sts in rib, then yrn, k2tog, then * work 9 (9: 10) sts, yrn, k2tog; rep from * 2 (2: 3) times, then cont in rib to end.

Work a further 2 rows in col C.

Change to col B, and work 2 rows.

Bind off all sts in rib, and fasten off securely.

Sewing together

❀ Measure 4¼ (4¾: 5¼) in [11 (12: 13) cm] down each side edge from the shoulder seam, and mark with pins.

❀ Stitch the armhole edge of each sleeve in position between the marked points.

❀ Join side and sleeve seams.

❀ Weave in all loose ends on the reverse.

❀ Sew buttons onto the front band to correspond with buttonholes.

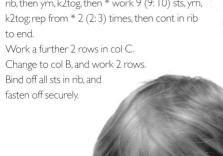

Outfits

Frog Suit with Hood

This all-in one outfit will keep baby snug as a bug—or amphibian—in a rug from head to toe, and the hood even has soft knitted frog eyes. Rows of knitted bobbles along the sleeves and hood add an irresistible tactile texture to the knit, but because the yarn used is very soft the bobbles won't feel lumpy against your baby's skin.

CHECKLIST

YOU WILL NEED
- pair of size 3 (3.25 mm) needles
- pair of size 6 (4 mm) needles
- size 3 (3.25 mm) circular needle
- 5 (6 : 7) 2 oz (50 g) balls light worsted knitting yarn in color A (green)
- oddment of light worsted knitting yarn in color B (white)
- oddment of light worsted knitting yarn in color C (black)
- tape measure
- stitch holders
- bodkin
- 17 small green buttons
- small amount of soft toy filling, approximately ½ oz (15 g)

TO FIT SIZES
0–3 months: chest 16 in (41 cm)
3–6 months: chest 18 in (46 cm)
6–12 months: chest 20 in (51 cm)

GAUGE
22 stitches and 30 rows to 4 in (10 cm), measured over stockinette stitch, using size 6 (4 mm) needles

SPECIAL ABBREVIATION
(see page 19 for standard abbreviations)
mb—make bobble.
Work to bobble position; purl into the next stitch, then knit into the same stitch. Repeat once more, then purl once. You will have made five extra stitches.
Use the tip of the left-hand needle to pass the first four extra stitches over the last to form the looped bobble. Work to next bobble position, and repeat.

Back
LEGS (MAKE 2 ALIKE)
Using size 3 (3.25 mm) needles and col A, cast on 16 (16 : 18) sts.
Work in k1, p1 rib for 1¼ in (3 cm), ending with a rs row.
Increase row with ws facing: rib 4 (2 : 3), then *m1, rib 1 st; rep from * to last 3 (2 : 2) sts, m1, then rib to end. (26 [29 : 32] sts.)
Change to size 6 (4 mm) needles, and cont in st st until work measures 8 (8¾ : 9½) in [20 (22 : 24) cm] from cast-on edge, ending with a ws row.
Transfer sts to a stitch holder.

BODY
Join legs to form body: work across sts from one leg, then work sts held on stitch holder from the other leg.
Cont in st st on these 52 (58 : 64) sts until work measures 8½ (9 : 9½) in [22 (23 : 24) cm] from the crotch join, ending with a ws row.
RAGLAN DECREASE
Bind off 3 sts at beg of next 2 (2 : 2) rows **, then dec 1 st at both ends of next and every alt row until there are 18 (20 : 22) sts, ending with a ws row.
Leave sts on a stitch holder.

Front
Work as back to **.
DIVIDE FOR FRONT OPENING
With rs facing, begin raglan shaping as follows: dec 1 st, knit 18 (21 : 24) sts, turn, and place the rem sts on a stitch holder. Work 1 row in st st.
Cont dec 1 st at same end of next and every alt row until there are 11 (12 : 15) sts.
Work 1 row in st st.

NECKLINE SHAPING

With rs facing, dec 1 st, work to last 2 sts, dec 1 st.
Dec 1 st at neck edge of next 3 (4:5) rows, while continuing the raglan shaping at the armhole edge. There are now 5 (4:6) sts.
Dec 1 st at armhole edge only on rs rows until 2 sts rem.
Place rem 2 sts on a stitch holder.
Slip the sts for the right front from the stitch holder onto your needle, and rejoin col A.
Bind off the first 6 sts, then cont following pattern instructions to make the right front section, remembering to reverse the raglan and neckline shapings.
Place rem 2 sts on a stitch holder.

Sleeve (make 2 alike)

Using size 3 (3.25 mm) needles and col A, cast on 26 (29:31) sts.
Work in k1, p1 rib for 1¼ in (3 cm) ending with a rs row.

INCREASE ROW WITH WS FACING

First size: rib 3, then *m1, rib 3; rep from * to last 2 sts, inc 1 st, then rib to end. (34 sts.)
Second and third sizes: rib (3:4), *inc 1 st, rib 3; rep from * to last (2:3) sts, inc 1 st, rib to end.
There are now 34 (38:40) sts.
Change to size 6 (4 mm) needles, and begin patt as follows:
Cont in st st for 4 rows.
Next row (bobble row): with rs facing, work 4 (6:7) sts *mb, work 4 sts; rep from * to last 0 (2:3) sts, k0 (2:3).
Work 5 rows, then work bobble row, keeping bobbles in same position vertically.
Cont in patt.

Inc 1 st at both ends of 2nd (2nd:2nd) row, then at both ends of every foll 6th (10th:10th) row until you have 40 (44:48) sts. Work 5 (7:9) rows.

RAGLAN DECREASE

Bind off 3 sts at beg of next 2 rows, then dec 1 st at both ends of next and every alt row until 6 sts remain.
Leave rem 6 sts on stitch holder.

Hood

With rs facing, using size 6 (4 mm) needles and col A, pick up and knit 10 (12:14) sts up right front neck, k across sts on front and first sleeve stitch holders, across back neck work *k1, m1; rep from * to last st, k1, k across sts on second sleeve and front stitch holders, then pick up and k10 (12:14) sts down left front neck. (71 [79:87] sts.)
Purl 1 row.
Cont in st st until hood measures 7 (7½:8) in [18 (19:20) cm], ending with a ws row, then bind off 22 (26:30) sts at beg of next 2 rows.
With rs facing, cont on rem sts and patt as follows:
Cont in st st for 4 rows.
Next row: with rs facing, work 3 (3:4) sts *mb, work 4 sts ; rep from * to last 4 (4:4) sts, mb, work to end.
Work 5 rows, then work bobble row, keeping bobbles in same position vertically.
Cont in patt for a further 4½ (5¼:6) in [11 (13:15) cm], ending with a ws row.
Bind off all sts, and fasten off securely.
Using a bodkin and col A, join hood seams.

Button band and buttonhole band for front opening and hood

Using a size 3 (3.25 mm) circular needle, pick up and knit 17 (19:19) sts along right front opening to neck, then 42 (46:50) sts along right side of hood to seam, 27 (27:27) sts across hood center front to other seam, 42 (46:50) sts down left side of hood, and 17 (19:19) sts along left front opening.

Work in k1, p1 rib for 3 rows.

Buttonhole row: Rib 3 sts, *yrn, k2tog, rib 4; rep from * another 2 times, then rib to end.

Rib for 3 more rows, then bind off all sts in rib, and fasten off securely.

Button band and buttonhole band for leg opening

BUTTON BAND

With rs facing, using size 3 (3.25 mm) needles and col A, pick up and knit 45 (51:57) sts evenly along inside leg edge of back to crotch, beg at the ankle rib of the left leg, then pick up and knit 46 (52:58) sts from crotch to the edge of the right ankle rib. Work in k1, p1 rib for 7 rows, then bind off all sts in rib, and fasten off securely.

BUTTONHOLE BAND

With rs facing, using size 3 (3.25 mm) needles and col A, pick up and knit 45 (51:57) sts evenly along inside leg edge of front to crotch, beg at the ankle rib of the right leg., then pick up and knit 46 (52:58) sts from crotch down to the edge of the left ankle rib. Work in rib for 3 rows.

Buttonhole row: Rib 4, *yrn, k2tog, rib 5 (6:7); rep from * to last 4 sts, yrn, k2tog, rib to end. Rib 3 more rows, then bind off all sts in rib, and fasten off securely.

Eyes and eyelids

(make 2 of each)

Using size 3 (3.25 mm) needles and col A for eyelids (col B for eyes), cast on 18 (24:30) sts.

Purl 1 row, then cont in st st for 6 (10:12) rows.

Next row: *k1, k2tog; rep from * to end.

Break off yarn, then draw it through the rem sts, pull together tightly, and fasten off securely.

Nostrils

(make 2)

Using size 3 (3.25 mm) needles and col A, cast on 15 (18:21) sts.

Purl 1 row, then cont in st st for 6 (8:10) rows.

Next row: *k1, k2tog; rep from * to end.

Break off yarn, then draw it through rem sts, pull together tightly, and fasten off securely.

Sewing together

✿ Join raglan, sleeve and side seams. Weave in all loose ends neatly on the reverse.

✿ Overlap the bands and sew the lower edges to the bound-off edge at the center front opening.

✿ Sew buttons onto lower left front side of button band to correspond with buttonholes.

SEWING TOGETHER EYES AND EYELIDS

✿ Join eye seam, and stuff each with a small amount of toy filling. Sew the cast-on edges to the hood at the end of the seam near the crown. Take an eyelid, and wrap it around the back part of the eye, so that the cast-on edge forms the lid around the eye. Sew the other edge to the hood around the base of the eye.

SEWING TOGETHER NOSTRILS

✿ The cast-on edge represents the opening of each nostril; sew the other edge to the hood close to the seams at the front.

✿ Weave in all loose ends neatly on the reverse. Finally, use a small amount of yarn in col C to make large stitches at the front of each eyeball to represent pupils.

Cow Suit with Horned Hat

"With a moo-moo here and a moo-moo there!" Here we have a classic black-and-white all-in-one suit, complete with horned hat and cute little flower-buttoned front fastening. The black patches are knitted using the intarsia technique (see page 21), which ensures that there are no loops or floats of yarn on the reverse side of the garment in which tiny fingers could get caught.

CHECKLIST

YOU WILL NEED
- pair of size 3 (3.25 mm) needles
- pair of size 6 (4 mm) needles
- 3 (4:5) 2 oz (50 g) balls light worsted knitting yarn in color A (white)
- 1 (2:2) 2 oz (50 g) balls light worsted knitting yarn in color B (black)
- 1 (1:1) 2 oz (50 g) ball light worsted knitting yarn in color C (brown)
- tape measure
- stitch holder
- bodkin
- 4 small flower-shaped buttons for front opening
- 11 small white buttons for leg opening
- small amount of soft toy filling, approximately ½ oz (15 g)

TO FIT SIZES
- 0–3 months: chest 16 in (41 cm)
- 3–6 months: chest 18 in (46 cm)
- 6–12 months: chest 20 in (51 cm)

GAUGE
22 stitches and 30 rows to 10cm (4in), measured over stockinette stitch, using size 6 (4 mm) needles

Back

LEFT LEG
Using size 3 (3.25 mm) needles and col A, cast on 16 (16: 18) sts.
Work in k1, p1 rib for 1¼ in (3 cm), ending with a rs row.
Increase row with ws facing: rib 4 (2: 3), then *m1, rib 1 st; rep from * to last 3 (2: 2) sts, m1, then rib to end. (26 [29: 32] sts.)
Change to size 6 (4 mm) needles, and cont in st st, working left-hand 26 (29: 32) sts of chart for cow patches (on pages 108–109) up to crotch point, ending with a p row. Transfer sts to a stitch holder.

RIGHT LEG
Using size 3 (3.25 mm) needles and col A, cast on 16 (16: 18) sts.
Work in k1, p1 rib for 1¼ in (3 cm), ending with a rs row.
Increase row with ws facing: rib 4 (2: 3), then *m1, rib 1 st; rep from * to last 3 (2: 2) sts, m1, then rib to end. (26 [29: 32] sts.)

Change to size 6 (4 mm) needles, and cont in st st, working right-hand 26 (29: 32) sts of chart for cow patches (on pages 108–109) up to crotch point.

JOIN LEGS TO FORM BODY

Cont to follow pattern chart: work across all sts on needle, then work across all sts from stitch holder. Cont on these 52 (58: 64) sts until the uppermost black patch is completed.

Cont in st st and col A until work measures 8¼ (8¾: 9) in [21 (22: 23) cm] from crotch, ending with a p row.

RAGLAN SHAPING

Bind off 3 sts at beg of next 2 rows **, then dec 1 st at both ends of next and every alt row until there are 18 (20: 22) sts. Work 1 more row, then place sts on stitch holder for back neck band.

Front

Work as for back to **.

DIVIDE FOR FRONT OPENING

With rs facing, begin raglan shaping as follows: dec 1 st, k 18 (21: 24) sts, turn, and place rem sts on a stitch holder. Work 1 row.

Cont dec 1 st at same end of next and every alt row until there are 11 (12: 15) sts.

Work 1 row.

NECKLINE SHAPING

With rs facing, dec 1 st, work to last 2 sts, dec 1 st.

Dec 1 st at neck edge of next 3 (4: 5) rows, while continuing the raglan shaping at the armhole edge. There are now 5 (4: 6) sts.

Dec 1 st at armhole edge only on rs rows until 2 (2: 2) sts rem.

Place rem 2 sts on a stitch holder for neck band. Slip the sts for the right front from the stitch holder onto your needle, and rejoin col A yarn. Bind off the first 6 sts, then cont following pattern instructions to make the right front, remembering

to reverse the raglan and neckline shapings. Place rem 2 sts on stitch holder for neck band.

Sleeve (make 2 alike)

Using size 3 (3.25 mm) needles and col B, cast on 26 (29: 31) sts.

Work in k 1, p 1 rib for 1¼ in (3 cm), ending with a rs row.

INCREASE ROW WITH RS FACING

1st size: rib 3, *m 1, rib 3; rep from * to last 2 sts, m 1, then rib to end. (34 sts.)

2nd and 3rd sizes: rib (3: 4), *m 1, rib 3; rep from * to last (2: 3) sts, m 1, rib to end. (38: 40 sts.)

Change to size 6 (4 mm) needles, and cont in st st, following pattern chart for sleeve, and working shaping as follows:

Inc 1 st at both ends of 7th (9th: 9th) row, then at both ends of every foll 6th (6th: 10th) row until there are 40 (46: 48) sts. Cont straight from chart to raglan shaping, ending with a p row.

RAGLAN SHAPING

Bind off 3 sts at beg of next 2 rows, then dec 1 st at both ends of next and every alt row until 6 sts rem.

Leave rem 6 sts on stitch holder for neck band.

Button band and buttonhole band for front opening

BUTTON BAND

With rs facing, using size 3 (3.25 mm) needles and col A, beg at base of opening, and pick up and knit 17 (19: 19) sts evenly along right front opening. Work in k 1, p 1 rib for 7 rows, then, with rs facing, bind off all sts, and fasten off securely.

BUTTONHOLE BAND

With rs facing, using size 3 (3.25 mm) needles and col A, beg at center front neck edge, and pick up and knit 17 (19: 19) sts evenly along left front opening.

Work in k 1, p 1 rib for 3 rows.

Buttonhole row: Rib 2 (4: 4) sts, *yrn, k2tog, rib 3; rep from * to end.

Work in rib for 3 rows, then, with rs facing, bind off all sts, and fasten off securely.

Neckband

With rs facing, using size 3 (3.25 mm) needles and col A, pick up and knit 6 sts evenly across the top of the front button band and 6 sts up right front neck, then knit across 2 sts held on stitch holder from right front neck, one sleeve, back neck, and the other sleeve and 2 sts held on stitch holder from left front neck. Now pick up and knit 6 sts down left front neck and 6 sts evenly across the top of the front buttonhole band. (58 [60: 62] sts.)

Work in p 1, k 1 rib for 3 rows.

Buttonhole row: Rib to last 5 sts, k2 tog, yrn, rib 3.

Work 3 rows in rib.

Bind off all sts in rib, and fasten off securely.

Button band and buttonhole band for leg opening

BUTTON BAND

With rs facing, using size 3 (3.25 mm) needles and col A, pick up and knit 39 (45: 51) sts evenly along inside leg edge of back to crotch, beg at the ankle rib of the left leg, then pick up and knit 40 (46: 52) sts from crotch to the edge of the right ankle rib.

Work in k 1, p 1 rib for 7 rows, then bind off all sts in rib, and fasten off securely.

BUTTONHOLE BAND

With rs facing, using size 3 (3.25 mm) needles and col A, pick up and knit 39 (45 : 51) sts evenly along inside leg edge of front to crotch, beg at ankle rib of right leg, then pick up and knit 40 (46: 52) sts from crotch down to edge of left ankle rib. Work in k 1, p 1 rib for 3 rows.

Buttonhole row: Rib 3 (4: 5), *yrn, k2tog, rib 5 (6: 7); rep from * to last 6 (7: 8) sts, yrn, k2tog, rib to end. Work 3 more rows in rib, then bind off all sts in rib, and fasten off securely.

Sewing together suit

✿ Overlap the front opening bands, and sew the lower edges to the bound-off edge of the front opening. Using a bodkin and col A, join raglan, side, and sleeve seams.

✿ Sew on 4 flower buttons to correspond with front opening buttonholes and 11 small white buttons to correspond with buttonholes along leg openings.

Horned hat

Using size 3 (3.25 mm) needles and col A, cast on 21 (25: 29) sts; now introduce col B and cast on a further 50 (53: 56) sts. There are now 71 (78: 85) sts in total.

Work in k1, p1 rib for ¾ (1¼: 1½) in (2 [3: 4] cm), working in both colors using the intarsia method (see page 21) and ending with a ws row.

With rs facing, change to size 6 (4 mm) needles, and work all rows of Hat chart on page 109, ending with a p row.

CROWN SHAPING

Cont in A.

With rs facing, begin crown dec as follows:

1st row: k1, *k2tog, k5; rep from * to end.

2nd and every alt row: purl all sts.

3rd row: k1, *k2tog, k4; rep from * to end.

5th row: k1, *k2tog, k3; rep from * to end.

7th row: k1, *k2tog, k2; rep from * to end.

9th row: k1, *k2tog, k1; rep from * to end.

11th row: k1, *k2tog; rep from * to end.

There are 11 (12: 13) sts rem.

Break off yarn, then draw it through the rem sts, pull together tightly, and fasten off securely.

Horn (make 2)

NOTE: The abbreviation "m1" means make an extra stitch by picking up and knitting the loop between stitches. This makes a decorative hole (see page 18).

Using size 6 (4 mm) needles and col C, cast on 3 sts.

1st row: k1, m1, k1, m1, k1.

Next row and every alt row: purl all sts.

3rd row: k2, m1, k1, m1, k2.

5th row: k3, m1, k1, m1, k3.

7th row: k4, m1, k1, m1, k4.

9th row: k5, m1, k1, m1, k5.

Cont inc 1 st either side of the central stitch until you have 21 sts.

Cont in st st until work measures 4¼ in (11 cm), ending with a ws row.

Bind off all sts, and fasten off securely.

Sewing together hat

✿ Using a bodkin and matching yarn, sew the hat seam, then weave in all tails of yarn neatly on the reverse. Join horn seams and stuff lightly.

✿ To position and sew the cow horns in place, put the hat on a head-sized bowl or similar object. Pin each horn into position, then sew the cast-on edge securely to the hat using yarn in col C.

Pirate Suit and Hat

This pirate's seafaring ensemble, complete with skull and crossbones motif on the hat, would certainly send shivers through everyone's timbers at a costume party. If you take away the characteristic hat, the striped sweater with a colorful collar looks chic and smart, and suitable for all kinds of daytime activities. If costume is baby's thing, you could also knit the pattern in black and yellow stripes to make a buzzy bee outfit. The tunic and leggings have a rolled edge at cuff and hem.

CHECKLIST

YOU WILL NEED
- pair of size 3 (3.25 mm) needles
- pair of size 6 (4 mm) needles
- 2 (3:3) 2 oz (50 g) balls light worsted knitting yarn in color A (white)
- 4 (5:5) 2 oz (50 g) balls light worsted knitting yarn in color (black)
- 1 (1:1) 2 oz (50 g) ball light worsted knitting yarn in color C (red)
- 20 in (50 cm) of ¼ in (6 mm) wide elastic
- tape measure
- stitch holders
- bodkin
- large safety pin
- sewing needle
- black sewing thread
- 4 white buttons for shoulder opening
- skull and crossbones patch for hat
- waist length of 1 in (2.5 cm) elastic for leggings
- 2 clear snap fasteners

TO FIT SIZES
0–3 months: chest 16 in (41 cm)
3–6 months: chest 18 in (46 cm)
6–12 months: chest 20 in (51 cm)

PATTERN
Worked in st st stripes: 4 rows col B, 4 rows col A

GAUGE
22 stitches and 30 rows to 4 in (10 cm), measured over stockinette stitch, using size 6 (4 mm) needles

Pirate top (Back)

Using size 3 (3.25 mm) needles and col A, cast on 53 (59:65) sts.

Knit 1 row.

Purl 1 row.

Cont in st st for 4 more rows.

With rs facing, work in k1, p1 rib for 1¼ in (3 cm), measured from beg of rib, ending with a ws row.

Change to size 6 (4 mm) needles and col B, and cont in st st and stripe patt until work measures 9 (10¾: 12) in [23 (27: 31) cm] from beg of rib, ending with a ws row.

SHOULDER SHAPING

With rs facing, bind off 8 (9: 10) sts at beg of next 2 rows, then 9 (10: 11) sts at beg of foll 2 rows.

Slip rem 19 (21:23) sts onto a stitch holder for back neck.

Front

Using size 3 (3.25 mm) needles and col A, cast on 53 (59:65) sts.

Knit 1 row.

Purl 1 row.

Cont in st st for 4 more rows.

With rs facing, work in k1, p1 rib for 1¼ in (3 cm), measured from beg of rib, ending with a ws row.

Change to size 6 (4 mm) needles and col B, and cont in st st and stripe pattern until work measures 7 (8¾: 10¼) in [18 (22:26) cm] from cast-on edge, ending with a ws row.

NECKLINE SHAPING

With rs facing, work 22 (24:26) sts, turn, and continue on these sts to make left front. Slip rem sts onto a stitch holder.

Dec 1 st at beg of next and at same edge of foll 4 rows. (17 [19:21] sts.)

Cont without shaping until work measures 8¼ (9¾: 11½) in [21 (25:29) cm] from cast-on edge, ending with a ws row.

SHOULDER SHAPING

With rs facing, bind off 8 (9:10) sts at beg of next row. Work 1 row, then bind off rem 9 (10:11) sts, and fasten off securely.

RIGHT FRONT

Slip 9 (11:13) sts at center front onto a stitch holder for front neck.

Rejoin yarn, then cont on rem sts, following neckline shaping at neck edge as before, then cont without shaping until work measures 9 (10¾: 12) in [23 (27:31) cm] from beg of rib, ending with a rs row.

SHOULDER SHAPING

With ws facing, bind off 8 (9:10) sts at beg of next row. Work 1 row, then bind off rem 9 (10:11) sts, and fasten off securely.

Sleeve (make 2 alike)

Using size 3 (3.25 mm) needles and col A, cast on 33 (35:37) sts.

Knit 1 row.

Purl 1 row.

Cont in st st for 4 more rows.

Work in k1, p1 rib for 1¼ in (3 cm), ending with a ws row.

With rs facing, change to size 6 (4 mm) needles and col B, and cont in st st and stripe patt.

SLEEVE SHAPING

Inc 1 st at both ends of next and every foll 4th row until there are 45 (49:53) sts.

Cont without shaping until work measures 6 (6¾: 8) in [15 (17:20) cm] from beg of rib, ending with a ws row.

ARMHOLE SHAPING

With rs facing, bind off 9 (10:11) sts at beg of next 4 rows.

Bind off rem 9 sts, and fasten off securely.

Shoulder bands and collar

Join right shoulder seam.

BUTTON BAND

With rs facing, using size 3 (3.25 mm) needles and col A, pick up and knit 17 (19:21) sts evenly across the left back shoulder edge.

Work in k1, p1 rib for ¾ in (2 cm), ending with a ws row.

With rs facing, bind off all sts.

BUTTONHOLE BAND

With rs facing, using size 3 (3.25 mm) needles and col A, pick up and knit 17 (19:21) sts evenly across the left front shoulder edge.

Work in k1, p1 rib for 3 rows.

Buttonhole row: Rib 2 (4:3) sts, *yrn, k2tog, rib 3 (3:4); rep from * twice more.

Cont in rib until band measures ¾ in (2 cm), ending with a ws row.

With rs facing, bind off all sts.

COLLAR

With rs facing, using size 3 (3.25 mm) needles and col A, pick up and knit 18 sts evenly from the top of the buttonhole band and down the left neck edge, then knit 9 (11: 13) sts held on stitch holder at front neck, pick up and knit 18 sts up right front neck, and knit 19 (21: 23) sts held on stitch holder at back neck.

Work in k1, p1 rib for 3 rows, ending with a ws row.

Next row: Rib 3, yrn, k2tog, rib to end.

Rib 3 rows.

Next row: Bind off 3 sts, k to last 3 sts, bind off 3 sts.

Change to col C and knit 1 row.

With rs facing, cont in st st for 18 rows.

Bind off all sts, and fasten off securely.

Sewing together the pirate top

✿ Overlap the buttonhole and button bands at the shoulder edge, and stitch the ribbed sections together.

✿ Measure 4¼ (4¾: 5¼) in [11 (12: 13) cm] down each side edge from the shoulder seam, then mark with pins.

✿ Stitch the armhole edge of each sleeve in position between the marked points.

✿ Join side and sleeve seams.

✿ Weave in all loose ends on the reverse.

✿ Sew on buttons to correspond with the buttonholes.

✿ Roll collar on to rs, overlap ends and sew 2 clear snap fasteners to edges.

Leggings (make 2 alike)

Using size 3 (3.25 mm) needles and col B, cast on 33 (35: 37) sts.

Knit 1 row.

Purl 1 row.

Cont in st st for 6 more rows.

Work in k1, p1 rib for 1¼ in (3 cm), measured from beg of rib and ending with a ws row.

Change to size 6 (4 mm) needles, and cont in st st.

LEG SHAPING

Inc 1 st at both ends of next and every following 3rd row until you have 57 (63: 67) sts, ending with a ws row.

CROTCH SHAPING

Cast on 3 sts at end of next 2 rows. (63 [69: 73] sts.)

Cont without shaping until work measures 7 (8: 8¾) in [18 (20: 22) cm] from crotch.

WAISTBAND

Change to size 6 (4 mm) needles, and work in k1, p1 rib for 3¼ in (8 cm), ending with a ws row.

Bind off all sts.

Sewing together the leggings

✿ Using a bodkin and col B, join crotch and inside leg seams.

✿ Fold the ribbed waistband in half, and slip stitch the top edge to the reverse side of the last stocking stitch row. Leave a small gap through which to insert the elastic.

✿ Cut a length of elastic to fit around the child's waist, allowing approximately 1 in (2.5 cm) extra for joining.

✿ Thread the elastic through the casing using a large safety pin. Stitch the ends of the elastic securely together, then slip stitch the gap in the casing closed.

Pirate hat
FRONT BRIM

Using 3 (3.25 mm) needles and col B, cast on 73 (77: 81) sts.

Knit 3 rows.

With rs facing, work in k1, p1 rib for 2 rows.

With rs facing, begin decrease as follows:

Next row: rib 34 (36: 38) sts, k2tog, k1, k2tog, rib 34 (36: 38) sts.

Next and every alt row: rib all sts.

Next row: rib 33 (35: 37) sts , k2tog, k1, k2tog, rib 33 (35: 37) sts.

Cont in this way until there are 41 (45: 49) sts.

* Cast on 15 (17: 18) sts at beg of next row and 15 (16: 18) sts on foll row. There are now 71 (78: 85) sts.

Cont in rib for a further 1¼ in (3 cm), ending with a rs row.

Change to size 6 (4 mm) needles and beg with a k row. Cont in st st until work measures 4 (4½: 4¾) in (10 [11: 12] cm) from *, ending with a purl row.

CROWN SHAPING

With rs facing, begin crown dec as follows:

1st row: k1, *k2tog, k5; rep from * to end.

2nd and every alt row: purl all sts.

3rd row: k1, *k2tog, k4; rep from * to end.

5th row: k1, *k2tog, k3; rep from * to end.

7th row: k1, *k2tog, k2; rep from * to end.

9th row: k1, *k2tog, k1; rep from * to end.

11th row: k1, *k2tog; rep from * to end.

There are now 11 (12: 13) sts remaining.

Break off yarn, draw it through the last sts, pull together tightly, and fasten off securely.

Sewing together the pirate hat

✿ Using a bodkin and col B, join the hat seam and weave in all tails neatly on the reverse. Fold up the front brim, and slip stitch to the hat.

✿ Using matching thread and needle, stitch the skull and crossbones patch to the front brim.

Colorful Robot

This all-in-one suit has a button opening from top to bottom for easy access and diaper changing. Reverse stocking stitch welts at the armhole and knee add a colorful detail. Follow the chart on page 109 to work the pattern on the suit front. We used duplicate stitch for the decoration (see page 21), but if you are confident you can use the intarsia technique (page 21). Think carefully about positioning before you begin.

CHECKLIST

YOU WILL NEED
- pair of size 3 (3.25 mm) needles
- pair of size 6 (4 mm) needles
- 4 (4:4) 2 oz (50 g) balls light worsted knitting yarn in color A (yellow)
- 2 (2:2) 2 oz (50 g) balls light worsted knitting yarn in color B (blue)
- 2 (2:2) 2 oz (50 g) balls light worsted knitting yarn in color C (red)
- bodkin
- stitch holders
- stiff card for making pom-poms (see page 22)

TO FIT SIZES
0–3 months: chest 16 in (41 cm)
3–6 months: chest 18 in (46 cm)
6–12 months: chest 20 in (51 cm)

GAUGE
22 stitches and 30 rows to 10 cm (4 in), measured over stockinette stitch, using size 6 (4 mm) needles

Hat

Using size 3 (3.25 mm) needles and col C, cast on 71 (78:85) sts.

Work in k1, p1 rib for 1¼ in (3 cm), ending with a ws row.

Change to size 6 (4 mm) needles, and cont in st st., keeping to color arrangement using the intarsia method (see page 21).

Work 33 (36:40) sts in col B, 5 (6:5) sts in col C, then 33 (36:40) sts in col A.

Cont in st st until work measures 4 (4¼:4¾) in [10 (11:12) cm] from cast-on edge, ending with a ws row.

CROWN SHAPING

1st row: k1, *k2tog, k5; rep from * to end.
2nd and every alt row: purl all sts.
3rd row: k1, *k2tog, k4; rep from * to end..
5th row: k1, *k2tog, k3; rep from * to end.
7th row: k1, *k2tog, k2; rep from * to end.
9th row: k1, *k2tog, k1; rep from * to end.
11th row: k1, *k2tog; rep from * to end.

You will now have 11 (12:13) sts rem. Break off yarn, then draw it through the rem stitches, pull together tightly, and fasten off securely.

Sewing together hat

Using a bodkin and matching yarn, join back seam.

Make 3 red, 1 yellow, and 1 blue pom-poms (see page 22). Stitch to hat in positions shown in picture at right.

Body

LEG (MAKE 2 ALIKE)

Using size 3 (3.25 mm) needles and col C, cast on 38 (44:50) sts.

Work k1, p1 rib for 1½ in (4 cm) ending with a ws row.

Change to size 6 (4 mm) needles, and cont in k1, p1 rib, inc 1st at both ends of next and foll alt rows until you have 48 (54:60) sts.

Work straight until work measures 3 (3½:4) in [8 (9:10) cm] from cast-on edge, ending with a ws row.

Change to col A, knit 1 row, then work in rev st st for 10 rows.

Next row: * p next st tog with corresponding loop from first row in A, rep from * to end.

Body (continued)

Change to col B, knit 1 row, then work in rev st st for 10 rows.

Next row: * p next st tog with corresponding loop from first row in B, rep from * to end. Change to col C, knit 1 row, then work in rev st st for 10 rows.

Next row: pick up and knit the loops from the third color change.

Change to col B, and work in st st without shaping for another 4½ (5½: 6¼) in [12 (14: 16) cm], ending with a ws row.

Place stitches on a spare needle, and make another leg the same.

JOINING THE CROTCH

Place all stitches on one needle, and cont in st st. Work first 48 (54: 60) sts, then cast on 6 sts,

work rem 48 (54: 60) sts, and cast on 3 sts. Work to end of next row, then cast on 3 sts. You will now have 108 (120: 132) sts. Cont in st st until work measures 7½ (8¼: 9) in [19 (21: 23) cm] from crotch, ending with a ws row.

DIVIDE FOR ARMHOLES

With rs facing, work 27 (30: 33) sts to form the right front, bind off 3 sts, work 48 (54: 60) sts to form the back, bind off 3 sts, and work rem 27 (30: 33) sts to form the left front. Use separate small balls of yarn to work the back and both fronts together on the same needles. Cont in st st without shaping until work measures 9½ (10¾: 12¼) in [24 (27: 31.5) cm] from crotch, ending with a purl row.

RIGHT FRONT

With rs facing, slip 6 sts onto a small stitch holder for front neck, then work 21 (24: 27) sts. Slip rem sts onto large stitch holder. Return to sts on needle, and dec 1 st at end and at same end of subsequent rows until 17 (20: 22) sts rem.

Cont in st st without shaping until work measures 11½ (12¾: 14¼) in [29 (32: 36.5) cm] from crotch.

Bind off all sts, and fasten off securely.

BACK

Return to the 48 (54: 60) sts on large stitch holder that form the back. Slip onto a needle. Cont in st st until work measures 11½ (12¾: 14¼) in [29 (32: 36.5) cm] from crotch. Bind off 17 (20: 22) sts at beg of next 2 rows. Slip rem sts onto stitch holder for back neck.

LEFT FRONT

Slip 6 sts for left front on stitch holder onto needle.

With rs facing, work to last 6 sts, then slip these sts onto stitch holder for front neck. Return to sts on needle, and dec 1st at beg of next and at same end of subsequent rows until

17 (20: 22) sts rem.

Cont in st st without shaping until work measures 11½ (12¾: 14¼) in [29 (32: 36.5) cm] from crotch.

Bind off all sts, and fasten off securely.

Sleeve (make 2 alike)

Using size 3 (3.25 mm) needles and col B, cast on 31 (31: 33) sts.

Work in k1, p1 rib for 1½ in (4 cm), ending with a ws row.

Change to size 6 (4 mm) needles. Cont in k1, p1 rib, inc 1st at both ends of every alt row until you have 43 (49: 55) sts

Cont straight until work measures 5 (6: 7) in [13 (15: 18) cm] from cast-on edge, ending with a ws row.

Change to col A , knit 2 rows, then work in rev st st, following shoulder shaping.

Next row: * work to last 10 sts, turn; rep from * to end.

Next row: * work to last 12 sts, turn; rep from * to end.

Next row: * work to last 14 sts, turn; rep from * to end.

Next row: * work to last 12 sts, turn; rep from * to end.

Next row: * work to last 10 sts, turn; rep from * to end.

Next row: * work to end, turn; rep from * to end.

Change to col C, knit 2 rows, then work in rev st st, following shaping.

Next row: * work to last 10 sts, turn; rep from * to end.

Next row: * work to last 12 sts, turn; rep from * to end.

Next row: * work to last 14 sts, turn; rep from * to end.

Next row: * work to last 12 sts, turn; rep from * to end.

Next row: * work to last 10 sts, turn; rep from * to end.

Next row: * work to end, turn; rep from * to end. Change to col B, knit 2 rows, then work in rev st st, following shaping.

Next row: * work to last 10 sts, turn; rep from * to end.

Next row: * work to last 12 sts, turn; rep from * to end.

Next row: * work to last 14 sts, turn; rep from * to end.

Next row: * work to last 12 sts, turn; rep from * to end.

Next row: * work to last 10 sts, turn; rep from * to end.

Next row: * work to end, turn; rep from * to end. Bind off all sts, and fasten off securely.

On ws of both sleeves, loosely stitch the loops together where the colors change, to form the shoulder folds or welts.

Front bands

BUTTON BAND
Using size 3 (3.25 mm) needles and col A, cast on 7 sts, and work in k1, p1 rib for 9 (10¼: 11¾) in [23 (26: 30) cm].
Slip sts onto stitch holder.

BUTTONHOLE BAND
Using size 3 (3.25 mm) needles and col A, cast on 7 sts, work k1, p1 rib for 1½ (1¾: 2) in [4 (4.5: 5) cm].
Next row: rib 3 sts, yrn, k2tog, work to end.
Next row: rib all sts. This forms the buttonhole.
Cont in k1, p1 rib, working a buttonhole every 1½ (1¾: 2) in [4 (4.5: 5) cm], until the buttonhole band matches the button band in length.

NECKBAND
Using a bodkin and col A, join shoulder seams. Work first 3 sts from buttonhole band, yrn, k2tog, work 2 sts, then work 6 sts held at front neck, pick up and k 10 (12: 14) sts evenly up the neckline edge to meet the shoulder seam, work across sts held at back neck, pick up and k 11 (13: 15) sts evenly around neckline edge, work 6 sts held at front neck, then 7 sts from button band. Work in k1, p1 rib across all sts for 1¼ in (3 cm), then bind off all sts, and fasten off securely.

Sewing together

✿ Join sleeve seams, then pin and stitch sleeves into armholes.

✿ Stitch button band and buttonhole band into position at center front.

✿ Make 6 yarn buttons using col C (see page 22). Stitch to button band to correspond with buttonholes.

✿ Overlap bands at lower edge, and stitch together.

✿ Join inside leg seams and crotch seams in one seam.

Decoration

Follow chart for decoration using duplicate stitch technique (see page 21).
Col B—blue
Col C—red

NOTE: SPACING
Begin top blue motif 5 (6: 7) rows down from the front neck.

TIPS FOR WORKING THE DECORATION
Count the rows carefully before you begin working the decoration. Mark the first (the bottom row) of the blue motifs with a pin. Work the blue motifs first, then add the red bands using the motifs as a guide to placement. Use our picture as a guide. Always work in the free ends as you go along—otherwise you are likely to get into a tangle on the reverse side. Work the decoration on one front first, then repeat in mirror image on the other side.

Templates

Templates

Use these templates to add the finishing touches to baby's Furry Bear Feet and Winged Booties. Simply trace the template outlines onto tracing or craft paper, cut out the pattern shapes, and use the paper templates to cut out the shapes in felt.

Furry Bear Feet

Sole template—cut soles in beige felt; cut pads in brown felt.

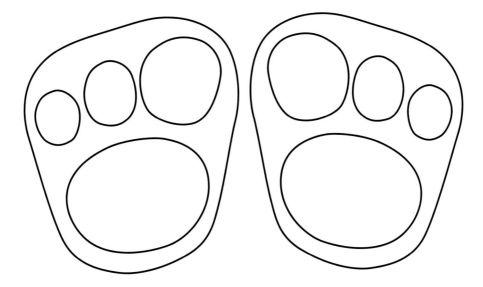

Winged Booties

Cut 2 in white felt.

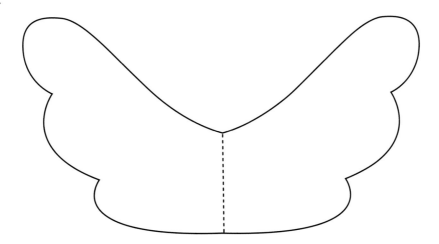

Pattern Charts

Here are the pattern charts for your wacky baby knits. Each square on the chart represents a stitch; begin at the bottom line, then start reading from right to left.

Baseball Jacket Sleeve

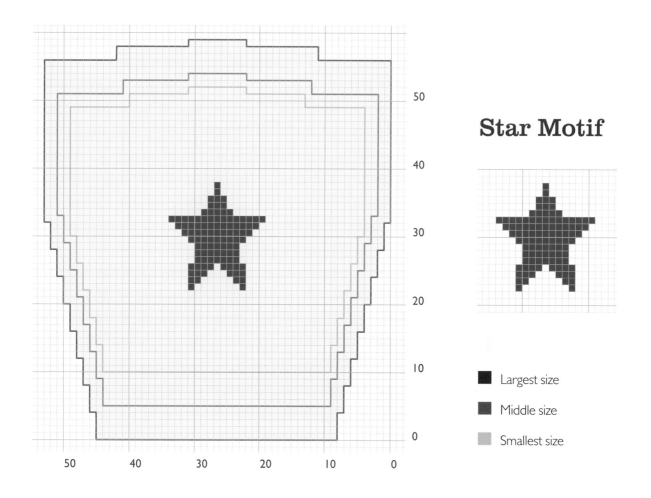

Star Motif

Largest size

Middle size

Smallest size

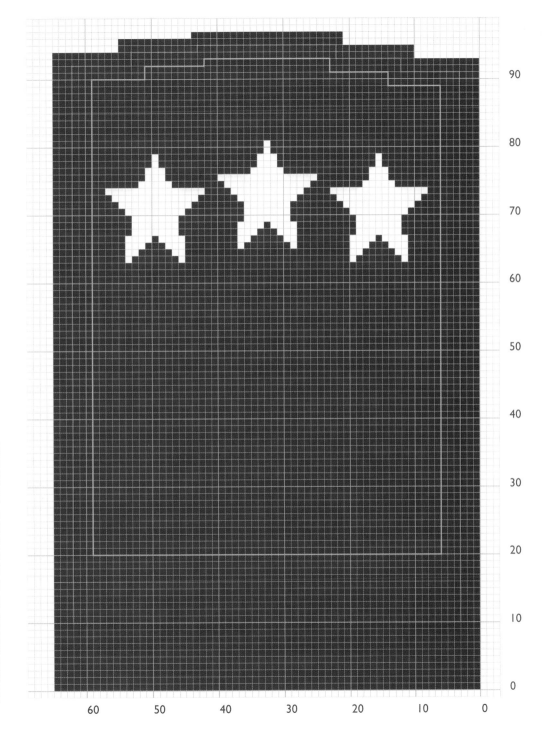

Baseball Jacket Back

Cow Suit Sleeve

Cow Suit Back

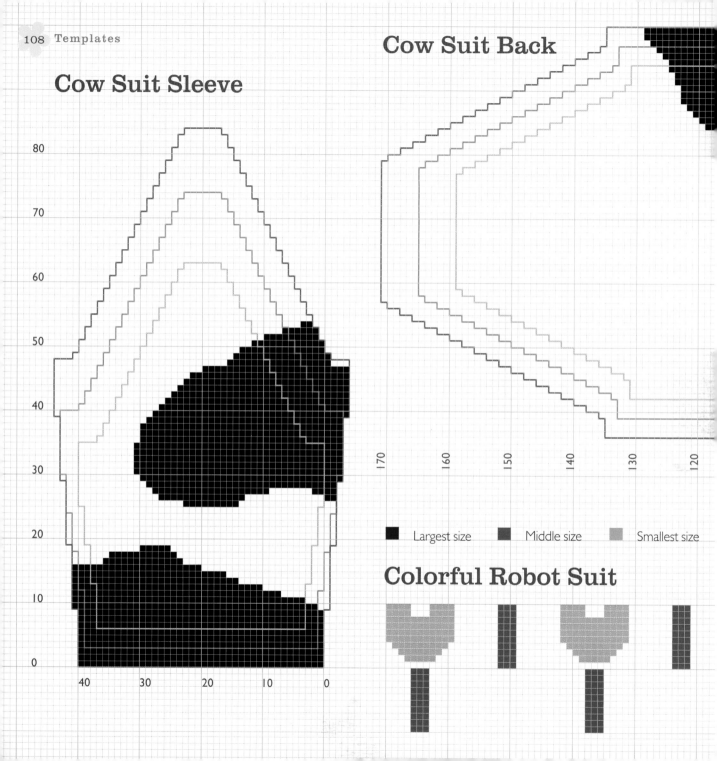

■ Largest size ■ Middle size ■ Smallest size

Colorful Robot Suit

Cow Suit Hat

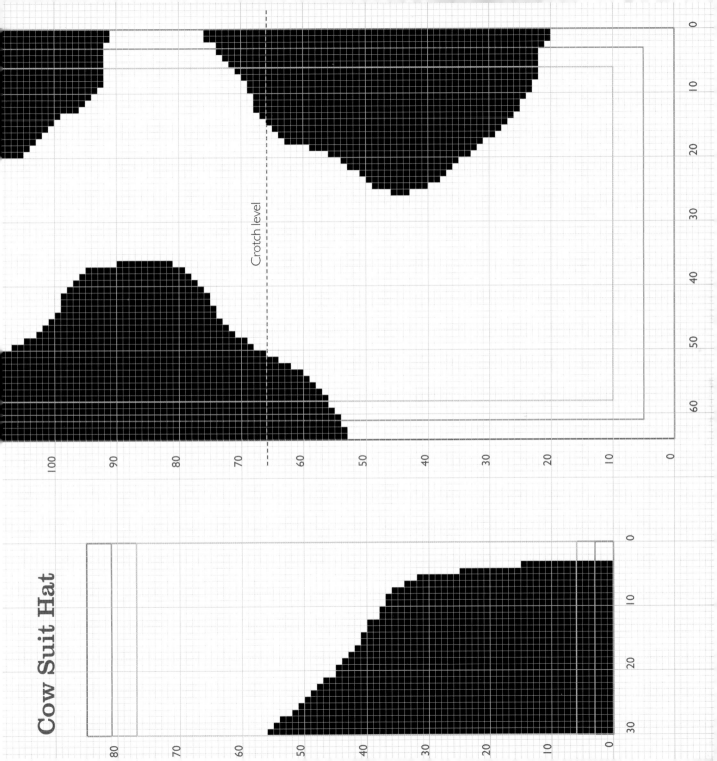

Crotch level

Glossary

BACKSTITCH SEAM A way of joining two knitted pieces by sewing a seam in backstitch by hand.

BIND OFF To end a piece of knitting so that the stitches remain secure and do not unravel or come undone.

BOBBLE A decorative cluster of stitches (see page 20).

CAST ON To create the first row of stitches on which to build a knitted piece.

DECREASE Decreasing the number of stitches on the needle is essential for creating pattern features and shaping the garment.

DUPLICATE STITCH An embroidery stitch worked by hand to resemble stockinette stitch and used to add different sections of color, particularly motifs or small patterns. Also known as "Swiss embroidery" or "darning" (see page 21).

FAIR ISLE A method of working in different-colored yarns without having to cut and join each color yarn for every color change.

FLAT SEAM A method of joining two knitted pieces by overstitching a seam by hand.

FLOAT A length of different-colored yarn that is carried along the back of a knitted piece when not being used.

GARTER STITCH A knitted piece worked solely in knit stitch.

GAUGE A method of counting stitches and rows, using a specified needle size, to ensure that the finished piece of knitting matches the length and width required in the pattern.

GRAFT To join two knitted pieces together in order to create a seam that is invisible.

INCREASE Increasing the number of stitches on the needle is essential for creating pattern features and shaping the garment.

INTARSIA A method for creating larger areas of color without using "floats" at the back (see page 21).

INVISIBLE SEAM A method of joining two pieces of knitting neatly and invisibly, to give a professional-looking finish (see page 21).

PICK UP AND KNIT This method works into the loops along the edge of a knitted piece and creates a row of stitches on which to create an edge for a collar, trim, or button band.

REVERSE STOCKINETTE The "wrong" side of a piece knitted in stockinette stitch. The purl (bumpy) side is used as the right side.

RIB The method of working knit and purl stitches alternately in order to create a ridged,

slightly elastic edge—often used for hems and cuffs.

SEWING IN TAILS A way of sewing dangling ends of yarn into a piece of work to neaten it after a color change or starting a new ball of yarn.

SHAPE/SHAPING Describes a way of shaping a knitted piece using the techniques of increasing and decreasing.

SLIP KNOT This is the first loop on the needle at the beginning of a row about to be cast on.

SLIPPED STITCH This is a stitch that is simply passed from one needle to another without being worked.

STOCKINETTE STITCH A knitted piece worked by alternating knit and purl rows. The knit (smooth) side is used as the right side.

Index

Acknowledgments

The publisher and author would like to thank test knitters Christine Cornwell and Liz Gunner, and pattern checker Susan Horan for their help on this book.

Many thanks also to the following beautiful baby models: William Anderton, Darcie Bonwick, Ellen Broadley, Lilia Cole, William Chapman, Jacob Kiwanuka, Mya Patel, Saran Patel, Luca Shanahan, Elise Standing, Amelia Stevens, Yasmin Travis, Amber Warnock, and Annabel Withington.